GRUESOME HARVEST

The Allies' Postwar War Against The German People

Ralph Franklin Keeling

If war should come, whichever side may claim ultimate victory, nothing is more certain than that victor and vanquished alike would glean a gruesome harvest of human misery and suffering.

—PRIME MINISTER NEVILLE CHAMBERLAIN
July 31, 1939, to the House of Commons

INSTITUTE FOR HISTORICAL REVIEW

Gruesome Harvest by Ralph Franklin Keeling

Originally published in 1947 by the Institute of American Economics (Chicago).

This IHR edition published June 1992 by the

Institute for Historical Review
P.O. 1306
Torrance, California 90505 USA

Manufactured in the United States of America

ISBN: 0-939484-40-4

Table of Contents

Dedication

This book is dedicated to those people in all lands who are ruled primarily by reason, rather than prejudice; who try to see events now the way they will be viewed a generation hence by sober historians; who try to identify the present distortion in public sentiment and understanding caused by total war and propaganda; who are willing to appraise the problems of peace in terms of national, rather than presumed personal self-interest; who do not ask others to follow rules and standards which they would not accept for themselves; who believe in equality before the law for whole peoples as for individuals; who recognize the injustice of condoning an act committed by one country while condemning the same act committed by another; who can see that an *a priori* picking of sides and choosing of favorites among nations without regard to their conduct is a repugnant form of racial or national discrimination; who strive for better human relations by helping overcome chauvinism, ethnocentrism, and persecution on any account; who respect human dignity and fundamental human rights; who have democratic faith in the simple honesty and soundness of the broad masses of people in all countries; who therefore believe that the people of no nation can be collectively condemned without condemning human nature itself; who sympathize with those millions of suffering, starving victims of total war wherever they may be; who seek the peace, prosperity, and happiness of all people, including those who live in our America—and our former enemies.

Publisher's Introduction to the 1992 Edition

Ralph Franklin Keeling's *Gruesome Harvest* was originally published in 1947. At the time it was written, a defeated, divided, and truncated Germany was occupied by the armies of its conquerors. Germany's cities were masses of rubble; its economy, a desperate scratching for subsistence; its people apathetic, cynical, demoralized. Within a short few years, however, a new Germany, or better two Germanies, had risen from the ruins. The currency reform of 1948 and the establishment of the Federal Republic of Germany in the west laid the groundwork for the most prosperous and the most "democratic" Germany in history. True, the German Democratic Republic in the Soviet zone to the east, and even more so divided Berlin, remained a symbol of division and a specter of the Cold War rivalry between the two nuclear superpowers. But the exhilarating events which began with the spontaneous, popular tearing down of the Berlin Wall on November 9, 1989, and culminated in the collapse of Communism and the reunification of Germany would seem to have relegated the brief, bitter years of postwar prostration to well-deserved oblivion.

Why, then, the republication of this book, with its focus on a little over two years of the postwar, with its lurid subtitle, *The Allies' Postwar War Against the German People.* Precisely because this shameful period, forgotten by the Americans, repressed by the Germans, deserves to be recalled as it actually happened, not as wishful thinking would have it.

Americans today, instructed by the standard academic and popular historians, associate America's postwar role in Germany above all with two events, each interpreted with maximum self-congratulation: the Nuremberg trials, by which Germany's Nazi leadership was brought to justice, and the Marshall Plan, whereby thanks to American generosity Germany's people were able to rebuild a free society and a free economy.

While our countrymen remember the Marshall Plan, however, they have forgotten its predecessor, the Morgenthau Plan, drawn up by America's wartime Secretary of the Treasury, Henry Morgenthau, and his closest advisor, Harry Dexter White, which aimed at the permanent destruction of Germany's industrial heart, with, as its ineluctable consequence, the death through starvation and disease of millions and tens of millions of Germans. As *Gruesome Harvest* makes clear, and as more recent studies have amply documented, Morgenthau and White's blueprint for genocide formed the basis of America's principal occupation policy directive, JCS 1067, from the outset of the occupation (for a recent survey, see "The Morgenthau Plan and the Problem of Policy Perversion," *The Journal of Historical Review*, Fall 1989).

In *Gruesome Harvest*, drawing copiously from the reports and the speeches of that minority of American journalists and statesmen who courageously opposed their government's initial postwar occupation policy, author Keeling amply demonstrates the effects of that policy in the two years which followed "V-E Day." Forcible expulsion of millions from their ancestral lands, and the theft of their homes and property; large-scale theft of capital and massive exploitation of slave labor; exploitation of women, from gang rape to black-market concubinage; censorship, book burning, concentration camps, *Sippenhaft* (arrest of kin), *Berufsverbot* (exclusion from one's profession), and other "Nazi" practices were the order of the day in occupied, "de-Nazified" Germany from 1945 to 1948.

Later studies, based on access to documentation unavailable to Keeling or to other writers in 1947, have substantiated and enlarged on the shocking revelations in *Gruesome Harvest.* Alfred de Zayas (*Nemesis at Potsdam*), James Bacque (*Other Losses*), Udo Walendy (*The Methods of Re-education*) and numerous other historians have furthermore amply confirmed the preponderant role that official U.S. policy played in these shameful events.

Several points on the Morgenthau plan and U.S. occupation policy in general deserve to be made here. First, the Morgenthau Plan, which was in fact largely crafted by Morgenthau's assistant

Preface

A year and a month after the Postdam Declaration was published, Secretary of State Byrnes suddenly left the Paris peace conference and went to Stuttgart where among the German people he attempted to justify and defend America's policy toward the defeated Reich.

This willingness to place a value on German public opinion marked a fundamental and welcome turning point in our official attitude, for previously we were carrying out our mission in Germany with utter disregard for what the Germans might think of it or us.

The change did not arise from any newly discovered fondness for our defeated subjects. Mr. Byrnes has put his finger on the real reason when he said: "It is not in the interest of the German people or in the interest of world peace that Germany should become a pawn or a partner in a military struggle for power between East and West."

That is precisely what had already happened. Belatedly, we had come to realize that while we were busily and blindly alienating the German people by carrying out one of the most brutal and terrifying peace programs ever inflicted on a defeated nation, Russia, who had been egging us on, was quietly preparing to come forward as their champion and to offer them an avenue of escape from us through the establishment of a unified, revived, and Communist Reich to be joined to the Soviet Union. This had been made clear by Molotov in July at Paris.

Germany is more than a mere pawn in the struggle for power between world ambitious Communist Russia and the West—she is the major prize. World Communism has long coveted Germany as the brightest jewel in its crown. The Kremlin knows and we know that all Europe would have to fall before the combined might of a union between Soviet Russia and a resuscitated Reich.

Such an eventuality cannot be tolerated by Britain who, with a hostile Europe at her back, would find her very existence threatened. Nor would we countenance such a threat to England, because treatment of the British Isles as our first line of defense in the Atlantic is one of the imperatives of our present foreign policy.

Union between Soviet Russia and a sovietized Germany would mean war. To prevent war, we must therefore prevent the fruition of Russia's design. Hence, it becomes necessary that we attract Germany to our side and keep her there.

The situation demands a thorough review of our German program, followed by whatever changes are required to establish a decent peace and prevent the Germans from feeling compelled by desperation to go over to the Russians.

The time has come for frank admission of past mistakes and courageous facing of hard facts. It is necessary for the American people to become thoroughly acquainted with what has been going on and to see to it that the proper corrective steps are taken and taken promptly.

This book is offered as a contribution to that end. It sets forth in plain terms just what has happened in Germany, because such knowledge is essential both to apprehend the German point of view and to become acquainted with the *status quo* from which we must proceed with remedial measures. It outlines the nature of Russia's design, together with a description of the mistakes we have made in falling so deeply into her trap. And finally it presents some suggestions for a peace settlement with Germany which would be at once just and permanent.

Chapter One

War Devastation

Devastation of the Reich by total warfare was alone enough to cast serious doubt on Germany's postwar ability to survive.

Never before in history have the life-sustaining resources of a nation been so thoroughly demolished. Returning from victory in Europe, General Bradley declared, "I can tell you that Germany has been destroyed utterly and completely."[1]

The demand for unconditional surrender had forced the desperate Germans to fight to the bitter end, until their cities had been pulverized into death-ridden rubble and their factories, railroads, canals, dams, power installations, communications, buildings, homes – all their exposed facilities – had been converted into heaps of twisted, smouldering ruins.

Allied fervor to destroy everything German had been expressed by General Eisenhower with the opening of the Roer drive.

"Our primary purpose," he declared, "is destruction of as many Germans as possible. I expect to destroy every German west of the Rhine and within that area in which we are attacking."[2]

Allied capacity to destroy became overwhelming after the American industrial colossus had been converted from peace-time to war production. American output soon surpassed that of all other belligerents in the war combined and became twice as great as the capacity of the doomed Axis.[3] Stunned by American power, Hermann Göring confessed to his Nuremberg prison guards: "The industrial genius of America is something of which no one dreamed."

A glimpse of America's smashing force when devoted to the grim business of mass production of death and destruction is provided by the following description written by a front line war correspondent:

> A cataclysmic blast of exploding, splintering steel rent the earth before us and it seemed like the world was coming to an end.
>
> The Americans were blasting out a path for a forward drive.
>
> Man and beast shuddered in their tracks. Whole towns were disintegrating. Life seemed to disappear from the scene. It was the most terrifying destructive force of warfare Germany has ever seen. And it was a symbol of what was to come as the U.S. 1st Army unloosed this shattering blow within the borders of Germany.
>
> For an hour and a half more than 2,000 bombers and hundreds of guns pounded the German countryside, making the earth dance before this mighty man-made force. When the heavies and mediums were not making the earth quake for miles around, our massed artillery was giving them hell out there. They were firing at an average rate of one round every 15 seconds, blasting every conceivable obstacle in our path. Minefields went up as though touched off by an electric switch . . .
>
> In the center of that frightful scene, the Germans were entrenched as a "human wall." They were dug in foxholes and inside houses of "fortified towns." Many died without knowing what had hit them.
>
> Having seen brave men and wild beasts crack as they do sometimes in the grip of a terrible earthquake, I could have sworn there would be no opposition when the zero hour came.
>
> Yet, when our tanks and doughboys went over the top after the barrage, as in the battle of Verdun, there were Germans still alive and they fought us with violence.[4]

Great though it was, the destruction resulting from ground fighting pales in comparison with that caused by our gigantic air raids. The two atom bombs dropped on Japan may have been more dramatic, but they could hardly have been more destructive than the millions of phosphorous, fire, and "blockbuster" bombs dropped on Germany. Near the end we were using 11-tonners which crews said caused their planes to bounce up over 500 feet when the huge 25-foot missiles were released, sending up "a tremendous pall of black smoke and a fountain of debris" which "dwarfed the terrific explosions of the six-ton 'earthquake' bombs."

To get the German economy off this dead center demands external assistance. And meanwhile the people, unable to produce the necessities of life for themselves, must either be allowed to die in masses or be given outside help until recovery has gone far enough to enable them once more to take care of themselves.

CHAPTER TWO

Extermination By Overcrowding

Germany's living space, even in 1937, was small for her heavy population and afforded important natural resources only in the form of farm lands and deposits of coal and potash. Her agricultural lands have been overworked by intensive cultivation for 1,000 to 2,000 years and her soil has been starved for fertilizer during and since the recent war. Even when plenty of fertilizer was available and her territory was intact, Germany was never able to produce more than 80 per cent of the food and other farm products needed to meet her domestic needs.[1] The rest had to be imported in exchange for coal and manufactured exports.

As her agricultural lands became overcrowded, Germany had resorted to manufacturing. By importing iron ore and exploiting her coal and potash resources to the utmost, she had built up the world's second largest steel and chemical industries which, in turn, formed the "workshop of Europe," raised the general European standard of living, and provided direct or indirect support for fully two thirds of her own population.

On account of destruction by total warfare and deliberate Allied policy, these industrial resources are now largely wiped out. Without them, over half of the German workers must resort to the soil as their only other means of life. Under the circumstances it is extremely doubtful that the land, even if all held in 1937 were left intact, could support the huge, now jobless, industrial population on even the barest subsistence level.

Without waiting to see, Germany's conquerors have ruthlessly stripped her of lands constituting 28 per cent of her living space, producing an even higher proportion of her food, and containing two of her three principal coal regions. To make matters still worse, they are expelling into the remaining Reich millions of Germans from the lost provinces, Poland, Hungary, Czechoslovakia, and elsewhere; are coddling a large population of "displaced persons" within stricken Germany; and, in the case of the Russians and French, are maintaining large armies of occupation which live off the land. Both the "displaced persons" and these occupation forces enjoy priority over the Germans by being able to make requisitions against them for whatever food and other items they need in order to live in comparative ease and luxury. The deplorable situation created by these actions can well be imagined.

The Atlantic Charter had promised:

> "No aggrandizement." No territorial changes that do not accord with the freely expressed wishes of the peoples concerned." "the right of all peoples to choose the form of government under which they live." "To all nations the means of dwelling in safety within their own borders." "A peace . . . which will afford assurance that all men in all lands may live out their lives in freedom from fear and want."

In their Yalta statement, the Big Three reaffirm their "faith in the principles of the Atlantic Charter" and say they uphold "the right of all people to choose the form of government under which they live." Yet in the same pronouncement they grant Russia the eastern half of Poland and as compensation promise the Poles "substantial accessions of territory" in eastern Germany—all without regard to "the wishes of the peoples concerned," "freely expressed" or otherwise.

Although Yalta prescribes that the exact amount of such territory Poland is to receive must await final adjudication at the peace conference, Russia at Potsdam confronted her two western allies with a territorial *fait accompli*. She had taken a third of East Prussia as her own permanent acquisition and had placed her Polish puppet in possession of all other German territory east of the Oder and Neisse Rivers. Even the drastic Morgenthau Plan had called for ceding Poland only the part of East Prussia not taken by Russia and the Upper Silesian coal and industrial region. But in addition to these areas, Poland had now possessed herself of German Posen, nearly all of Pomerania and Lower Silesia, and the

Potsdam calls for annulment of all Nazi laws which established discrimination on grounds of race and declares: "No such discrimination, whether legal, administrative or otherwise, shall be tolerated." Yet these forced migrations of German populations are predicated squarely on rank racial discrimination. The people affected are mostly wives and children of simple peasants, workers, and artisans whose families have lived for centuries in the homes from which they have now been ejected, and whose only offense is their German blood. How "orderly and humane" their banishment has been is now a matter of record.

Winston Churchill was not exaggerating when, in referring to the expulsions some three months after V-E Day, he informed the House of Commons:

> It isn't impossible that a tragedy on a prodigious scale is imposing itself behind the iron curtain which presently divides Europe.[4]

The conservative newletter, *Review of World Affairs*, quotes as follows from a confidential memorandum prepared by an eminent European economist:

> Since the end of the war about 3,000,000 people, mostly women and children and overaged men, have been killed in eastern Germany and south-eastern Europe; about 15,000,000 people have been deported or had to flee from their homesteads and are on the road. About 25 per cent of these people, over 3,000,000, have perished. About 4,000,000 men and women have been deported to eastern Europe and Russia as slaves . . . It seems that the elimination of the German population of eastern Europe—at least 15,000,000 people—was planned in accordance with decisions made at Yalta. Churchill had said to Mikolajczyk when the latter protested during the negotiations at Moscow against forcing Poland to incorporate eastern Germany: "Don't mind the five or more million Germans. Stalin will see to them. You will have not trouble with them: they will cease to exist."[5]

Dr. Lawrence Meyer, executive secretary of the Lutheran Church, Missouri Synod, after a tour of Germany stated:

> About 16,000,000 German refugees east of the Oder are being deported from their homes. It has been estimated that already 10,000,000 have been driven out. The human tragedy and suffering caused by this "Volkswanderung" are unparalleled in history. Hunger, cold, sickness, and death is the lot of millions. An authentic eye-witness report of the physical wretchedness of most of the refugees is pictured in the following:

"A large barge is slowly being towed across the Oder River. In it, lying on straw, are 300 children ranging from 2 to 14 years of age. There is hardly a sign of life in the whole group. Their hollow eyes, their swollen bellies, knees, and feet are telltale signs of starvation. These are merely the vanguard of hundreds of thousands – millions of homeless, shattered, hungry, sick, helpless, hopeless human beings fleeing westward – west of the Oder and Neisse Rivers.

"A trust in God – in his goodness and mercy – these are the only hope of Germany today. And thank God in many there is still faith in God against which the gates of hell have stormed in vain during the past decade."[6]

In describing the expulsions in Poland and Czechoslovakia, Russian officers told *Chicago Daily News* correspondents:

> The Poles have cleaned out all the Germans as far west as the Oder River, and now all that property is for any Poles who want it.
>
> The Czechs have taken care of the Germans in Sudetenland in their own way – and it's not pretty. They round them up, with only what they can carry, and start them moving.

Upon returning to his post as professor of political science at the University of Michigan, after serving 14 months as director of AMG's regional government coordinating office, Dr. James K. Pollock, in August, 1946, said most of the 2-1/4 million expellees from Hungary and Sudetenland are old women and children. He said:

> The Germans we are getting are mostly from the Sudetenland or Germans whose families had been living in Hungary for some 500 years. They come in perfectly frightful condition. They even took the women's wedding rings before they left. In many cases they have no clothes except those they are wearing.[7]

An officer would call at the door of the victims and order them to leave their home within a few hours, permitting them to take along 30 to 100 lbs. of luggage containing nothing of value which might help them in making a new start elsewhere. The property forcibly left behind would be confiscated by the state. Any able-bodied men found would be hustled off to slavery. The others would then start their perilous hegira to overcrowded Germany wholly without protection of law, subjected to every conceivable abuse, including robbery, beatings, rape and murder.

A dispatch in December, 1945, paints a picture of the plight of the exiles in the new Poland, where hundreds of thousands had been ousted from their homes and left to wander where they would. Former German cities like Breslau are described as almost depopulated of Germans, with Poles taking their place. The dispatch goes on to say:

> Hundreds of thousands of person in Poland are constantly on the move, restlessly seeking a spot where they can grub a living out of the war raged land. In every rail station and junction men, women, and children await transport. Clusters of human beings, almost hidden under loads of parcels and cans and other remnants of what must have been their homes, wait along the roads or in blasted villages for any transport that will carry them somewhere else. Life with its birth and death continues even in these nomadic streams and everywhere you see womenfold tending their sick or nursing babies.[8]

An eyewitness report of the arrival in Berlin of a train which had left Poland with exacly 1,000 refugees aboard reads:

> Nine hundred and nine men, women, and children dragged themselves and their luggage from a Russian railway train at Leherte station today, after 11 days travelling in boxcars from Poland.
>
> Red Army soldiers lifted 91 corpses from the train, while relatives shrieked and sobbed as their bodies were piled in American lend-lease trucks and driven off for interment in a pit near a concentration camp.
>
> The refugee train was like a macabre Noah's ark. Every car was jammed with Germans . . . the families carry all their earthly belongings in sacks, bags, and tin trunks . . . Nursing infants suffer the most, as their mothers are unable to feed them, and frequently go insane as they watch their offspring slowly die before their eyes. Today four screaming, violently insane mothers were bound with rope to prevent them from clawing other passengers.
>
> "Many women try to carry off their dead babies with them," a Russian railway official said. "We search the bundles whenever we discover a weeping woman, to make sure she is not carrying an infant corpse with her."[9]

New York *Daily News* correspondent Donald Mackenzie likewise reports from Berlin:

> In the windswept courtyard of the Stettiner Bahnhof, a cohort of German refugees, part of 12,000,000 to 19,000,000 dispossessed in East Prussia and Silesia, sat in groups under a driving rain and told the story of their miserable pilgrimage, during which more

> than 25 per cent died by the roadside and the remainder were so starved they scarcely had strength to walk.
>
> Filthy, emaciated, and carrying their few remaining possessions wrapped in bits of cloth they shrank away crouching when one approached them in the railway terminal, expecting to be beaten or robbed or worse. That is what they have become accustomed to expect.
>
> A nurse from Stettin, a young, good-looking blond, told how her father had been stabbed to death by Russian soldiers who, after raping her mother and sister, tried to break into her own room. She escaped and hid in a haystack with four other women for 4 days . . .
>
> On the train to Berlin she was pillaged once by Russian troops and twice by Poles . . . Women who resisted were shot dead, she said, and on one occasion she saw a guard take an infant by the legs and crush its skull against a post because the child cried while the guard was raping its mother.
>
> An old peasant from Silesia said . . . victims were robbed of everything they had, even their shoes. Infants were robbed of their swaddling clothes so that they froze to death. All the healthy girls and women, even those 65 years of age were raped in the train and then robbed, the peasant said.[10]

Precedent for these inhuman expulsions was set long before Potsdam in Romania where, according to a diplomatic report from Bucharest, 520,000 Romanian citizens of German ancestry, men between the ages of 17 and 45 and women between 18 and 30, were rounded up like slaves and deported to Soviet Russia. The document said "there were heart-rending scenes and many preferred suicide to an unknown fate in Soviet Russia."[11]

The United States had made its own direct contribution by ousting more than 16,000 people of German extraction from Latin American countries, obtaining permission to do so by pressure of various kinds applied from Washington, extraditing them without trial to this country, holding them here in concentration camps incommunicado and still without trial, and finally deporting them out of this hemisphere where many of them have been impressed into slavery by England and France.[12]

These wholesale expulsions of native populations are as reprehensible as anything the Nazis are accused of doing, and have caused deep resentment among all classes of Germans. Had America kept her skirts clean, and especially if she had denounced them, as she should have done, German respect for us would have soared. As matters stand, Germans blame us almost as much as the Russians and Poles. Our hands, too, are stained with the blood of millions of innocent victims of this savage, thoroughly un-American program.

Apart from the moral aspects of the matter, the dumping of all these millions of expropriated, helpless, people into what remains of wrecked Germany piles chaos upon chaos and helps convert the entire German nation into one vast Belsen or Buchenwald.

CHAPTER THREE

Pulling Down the Pillar of Labor

Allied attacks against German manpower have proceeded along three main fronts: enslavement, denazification, and physical incapacitation through undernourishment. Our present discussion will take up the first two of these, with starvation postponed for special treatment.

President Roosevelt on October 21, 1944, promised that "the German people are not going to be enslaved, because the United Nations do not traffic in human slavery." In the preceding month of Quebec, however, he had used strong pressure to obtain Mr. Churchill's acceptance of the Morgenthau Plan which called for "forced German labor outside Germany." *Pravda* writer Boris Izakov wrote that when in the following February at Yalta the proposal was advanced to force German workers to rebuild war-damaged areas, "President Roosevelt called this a healthy idea."[1] It was at this meeting that Mr. Roosevelt pressed the Morgenthau Plan and won Mr. Stalin's ominously ready acceptance.

Although at Potsdam it was solemnly promised again that "It is not the intention of the Allies to . . . enslave the German people," thousands of Germans had already been marched eastward into Russia's yawning slave camps. More that a month earlier, on June 29, 1945, the following had been published:

> German prisoners in Russian hands are estimated to number from four to five millions. When Berlin and Breslau surrendered, the long grey-green columns of prisoners were marched east downcast and fearful . . . toward huge depots near Leningrad, Moscow, Minsk, Stalingrad, Kiev, Kharkov, and Sevastopol. All fit

> men had to march some 22 miles a day. Those physically handicapped went in handcarts or carts pulled by spare beasts . . . They will be made to rebuild the Russian towns and villages which they destroyed. They will not return home until the work is completed.[2]

It has long been an open secret that Russia maintains under the direction of the NKVD (secret police) a vast army of Russian slaves, varying in number form 10-20 millions, mainly recruited as "political unreliables."[2] The presence and importance of this huge slave force explains, among other things, the profitability and frequency of Soviet Russia's many "purges": they are primarily a device for rounding up prisoners for enslavement. It is not surprising, therefore, that the Soviet Union should jump at the opportunity to enslave millions of defeated enemy civilians and soldiers and, to avoid special criticism, induce her allies to do likewise.*

A few crippled and ailing Germans who have survived the ordeal have been returned from the Russian slave camps to Berlin where American correspondents have obtained first hand accounts of what is happening. German Red Cross girls went at 9 a.m. on the morning of September 10, 1946, to meet a 20-car trainload of returning forced laborers. As the sealed cars were opened by the armed guards who had been riding on top, the girls were greeted with thin, scabby-faced men in rags begging for water or hysterically calling for help in removing the dead. A professional nurse told the story:

> They had been in the train almost a week traveling about 60 miles from Frankfurt-on-Oder. There had been deaths from starvation, not from starvation just during the ride, but from the hardships of

---

*When it was learned that the Soviets were impressing German civilian personnel for service in factories being removed to Russia, Britain and the United States protested. In reply the Russians produced a proclamation signed by Gen. Eisenhower a year earlier requiring that German authorities must carry out any measures of restitution, reinstatement, restoration, reparations, reconstruction, relief or rehabilitation as the Allied representatives might prescribe, to accomplish which the Germans must "provide such transporation, plant equipment and materials of all kinds, labor, personnel, specialists, and other services for use in Germany or elsewhere as the Allied representatives may direct." Since the document did not require four-nation agreement, the Russians are permitted by it to act unilaterally. After it was produced, Britain and the United States had to withdraw their protests.

> the trip after months of malnutrition in Russian labor camps. Almost all of the 800 or 900 in the train were sick or crippled. You might say they were all invalids. With 40 to 50 packed in each of those little boxcars, the sick had to sleep beside the dead on their homeward journey. I did not count them but I am sure we removed more than 25 corpses. Others had to be taken to hospitals. I asked several of the men whether the Russian guards or doctors had done anything on the trip to care for the sick. They said "No."
>
> I met only one alert, healthy man in the lot and I have seen him since. He was just a kid of 17. The boy told me that prisoners leaving Russian camps for Germany are searched to prevent any from smuggling mail for their comrades. Therefore, when one of them has been diagnosed as a hopeless invalid, in anticipation of discharge he will memorize the names and addressed of relatives to whom he can report for his fellow prisoners. He said only prisoners in special favor are able to mail postcards to their nearest of kin. This kid of 17 had memorized 80 names and addresses in Berlin of relatives of his prison friends. He found the buildings at most of the addresses in rubble, with the present whereabouts of the former occupants unknown, but he visited all 80 addresses in his first six days in Berlin.[4]

The daily diet in Russian slave camps is soup and lectures on the glories of Communism and the evils of western democracy. The slightest disobedience is penalized by such heavy work that a third of the culprits die within three weeks from exhaustion. A tenth of the slaves died during the first year, according to those who have returned.[5]

If prisoners released by the Russians as unfit for further forced labor happen to recuperate, they are re-impressed and sent back for more.[6] Moreover, able-bodied Germans we have released who have returned to their former homes in the Russian zone are arrested by the Russians and sent to the Soviet Union for enslavement, on the pretext that they have been rendered "politically unreliable" through exposure to British or American influences.[7] Refusal of released prisoners to return to the Russian zone has created a major problem, which France has attempted to meet by permitting the men to remain in France as a special class of citizens.

When the war ended, we enjoyed a decided advantage over the Russians in German esteem. Aware of the barbarities of the NKVD's treatment of slaves, German soldiers did their best to avoid falling into the hands of the Red armies, preferring instead to surrender to the British or Americans. German prisoners who were to be turned over to the Russians often committed suicide or tried to incapacitate themselves by slashing their bodies with knives, razors, or bits of glass.[8] Persistent reports coming from Russia, however, tell of large numbers of German prisoners joining the Red Army, after indoctrination in Communism, and justify the fear that ultimately the huge German prison army in Russia may be successfully converted into a potent military force which may someday be turned against the West.[9]

France, according to the International Red Cross, had 680,000 former German soldiers slaving for her in August, 1946. 475,000 of their number had been captured by the United States and later turned over to the French for forced labor.[10]

French treatment of her slave subjects is revolting to the civilized conscience. In an article entitled, "We Should Not Resemble Them," *Figaro* reveals:

> In certain camps for German prisoners of war . . . living skeletons may be seen, almost like those in German concentration camps, and deaths from undernourishment are numerous. We learn that prisoners have been savagely and systematically beaten and that some have been employed in removing mines without protection equipment so that they have been condemned to die sooner or later.
>
> People, of course, will point to the Gestapo tortures, the gas chambers and the mountains of human bodies found in the internment camps in Germany. But these horrors should not become the theme of sports competition in which we endeavor to outdo the Nazis . . . We have to judge the enemy, but we have a duty not to resemble him.[11]

Gathering his facts from numerous reliable sources, Louis Clair writes in *The Progressive* of "the horrible conditions in the French camps of German POW's." He says:

> In a camp in the Sarthe district for 20,000 prisoners, inmates receive 900 calories a day; thus 12 die every day in the hospital. Four to five thousand are unable to work at all any more. Recently trains with new prisoners arrived in the camp: several prisoners had died during the trip, several others had tried to stay alive by eating coal that had been lying in the freight train by which they came.
>
> In an Orleans camp, the commander received 16 francs a day per head or prisoner to buy food, but he spent only nine francs, so that

> the prisoners were starving. In the Charentes district, 2,500 of the 12,000 camp inmates are sick. A young French soldier writes to a friend just returned from a Nazi camp:
>
> "I watch those who made you suffer so much, dying of hunger, sleeping on cold cement floors, in no way protected from rain and wind. I see kids of 19, who beg me to give them certificates that they are healthy enough to join the French Foreign Legion . . . Yes, I who hated them so much, today can only feel pity for them."
>
> A witness reports on the camp in Langres: "I have seen them beaten with rifle butts and kicked with feet in the streets of the town because they broke down of overwork. Two or three of them die of exhaustion every week."
>
> In another camp near Langres, 700 prisoners slowly die of hunger; they have hardly any blankets and not enough straw to sleep on; there is a typhoid epidemic in the camp which has already spread to the neighboring village. In another camp prisoners receive only one meal a day but are expected to continue working. Elsewhere so many have died recently that the cemetery space was exhausted and another cemetery had to be built.
>
> In a camp where prisoners work on the removal of mines, regular food supplies arrive only every second day so that "prisoners make themselves a soup of grass and some stolen vegetables." All prisoners of this camp have contracted tuberculosis. Here and elsewhere treatment differs in no respect from the Nazi SS brutality. Many cases have been reported where men have been so horribly beaten that their limbs were broken. In one camp, men were awakened during the night, crawled out of there barracks and then shot "because of attempted escape."
>
> There are written affidavits proving that in certain camps commanding officers sold on the black market all the supplies that had been provided by American Army authorities; there are other affidavits stating that prisoners were forced to take off their shoes and run the gauntlet. And so on, and so on . . . These are the facts.[12]

After we had delivered the first 320,000 prisoners, the French returned 2,474 of them to us, claiming that we had given them weaklings. Correspondents described them as "a begger army of pale, thin men clad in vermine infested taters." All were pronounced unfit for work—three-fourths of them on account of malnutrition—and 19 per cent had to be hospitalized. Associated Press photographer Henry Griffin, who had taken pictures of the corpeses piled in all German concentration camps, including Buchenwald and Dachau, said of the men: "The only difference I can see between these men and those corpses is that here they are still breathing.[13]

Asked to investigate, the Red Cross reported the prisoners were receiving inhuman treatment. Upon our threat to stop further transfers the French protested that they must have more prisoners or suffer heavy financial loss. It then came out that the French Government was hiring the men out to French employers for which it collected regular union wages, an average of 150 francs per day per man. Out of this, the government paid each prisoner 10 francs, and stood their daily cost of upkeep of perhaps another 40 francs, leaving a daily net profit of 100 francs per slave. In the aggregate the French Government thus stood to make a profit of over 50 billion francs a year from its German slaves![14] No wonder it became upset when we threatened to stop handing them over.

When we resumed deliveries, we took pains to make sure that the prisoners were in satisfactory physical condition. The men would be lined up and examined, their mouths opened and inspected, their chest thumped, their joints tried, their eyes, ear and teeth looked over, as if they were horses being offered for sale. GI's witnessing this spectacle were overheard to remark: "Gee! I hope we don't ever lose a war."

In the summer of 1946 a hopeful development which may bring an end to the slave traffic in France put in its appearance. It began when prisoners newly arrived from American POW camps not only refused to work in French coal mines but persuaded prisoners already there to follow their example.[15] A month later some of the prisoners were freed and then hired to work at full union wages, frankly as a measure to increase output.[16] The experience proves that in this modern world at least men when free produce more abundantly and profitably than when enslaved.*

---

*On December, 5, 1946, it was announced that the American Government had requested the repatriation by October 1, 1947, of the 674,000 German POW's it had turned over to France, Belgium, The Netherlands, and Luxemburg. France had agreed to release its 620,000 of this number but gave no definite pledge of when they would be freed. The French Government also disclosed that the United States, in a Dec. 21, 1945, memorandum, expressly stipulated that the Germans captured by the American Army and handed over to France were chattels to be used indefinitely for forced labor as part of France's war reparations from Germany. Meanwhile reports continued to pour into the press that conditions in

Great Britain in August, 1946, according to the International Red Cross, had 460,000 German prisoners slaving for her,[17] and as in the case of France bringing in a handsome profit to the War Office. Upon embarking from our ports the prisoners were given to understand that they were being sent home; when they learned upon arrival in British or French ports that they were to be worked indefinitely as slaves, they became sullen. As one British officer said, "It takes us several weeks to bring them around where they will work hard."[18]

A British contractor employing German slaves for skilled work is reported to have remarked:

> When you see how well they do things and how awful our own Ministry of Works—we call the Ministry the O.C., short for organized chaos—messes things up, it makes you wonder how we ever won the war.[19]

Among other projects, the prisoners were forced to build in Kensington Gardens a British victory celebration camp to house 24,000 empire troops who marched in the Empire's Victory Day parade. One foreman remarked: "I guess the Jerries are preparing to celebrate their own downfall. It does seem as though that is laying it on a bit thick."[20]

The British Government nets over $250,000,000 annually from its slaves. The Government, which frankly calls itself the "owner" of the prisoners, hires the men out to any employer needing men, charging the going rates of pay for such work—usually $15 to $20 per week. It pays the slaves from 10 cents to 20 cents a day, depending on the character of the work required, plus such "amenities" as slaves customarily received in the former days of slavery in the form of clothing, food, and shelter.[21] The prisoners are never paid in cash, but are given credits, either in the form of vouchers for camp post exchange items or credits against the time when they will be liberated. In March 1946, 140,000 prisoners were working on farms, for which the Government collected $14 a week per prisoner, 24,000 on housing and bomb damage clearance, 22,000 on railroads, mostly as section hands, the

---

the French slave camps remained as bad or worse than before—starvation diets, little protection from the elements or disease, in filthy, vermin-infested quarters.

balance at odd jobs, such as digging weeds out of the Thames river or serving as menials for GI brides awaiting shipment to America.[22]

According to revelations by members of the British House of Commons, about 130,000 former German officers and men were held during the winter of 1945-46 in British camps in Belgium under conditions British officers have described as:

> . . . not much better than Belsen. The prisoners lived through the winter in tents and slept on the bare ground under one blanket each. They say they are underfed and beaten and kicked by the guards. Many have no underclothes or boots.[23]

In the summer of 1946 an increasing number of prisoners were escaping from British slave camps with British civilian aid. Accounts of the chases by military police are reminiscent of pre-Civil War pursuits of fleeing negro fugitives.[24] By mid-September public indignation had risen to such a pitch that the British War Office announced that plans were under way to release 15,000 slaves per month, with preference given those displaying "genuine democratic" convictions. Army officers and important Nazis would not be repatriated under the plan. However, promises were made to improve conditions in the camps.[25]

The official International Red Cross report in August 1946 showed that our own government, through its military branch in the German zone, was exacting forced labor from 284,000 captives, 140,000 of them in the occupation zone, 100,000 in France, 30,000 in Italy, and 14,000 in Belgium.[26]

Slave holdings of other countries, as reported by the Red Cross, were: Yugoslavia 80,000; Belgium 48,000; Czechoslovakia 45,000; Luxemburg 4,000; Holland 1,300.[27]

Keeping these millions of Germans away from their families is a direct attack against the German home and family, and in this respect serves only Communism. Still the tie that binds the men to their loved ones has remained strong. A dispatch from Geneva tells a touching story.

> Hundreds of tons of parcels shipped by German war prisoners in United States camps to relatives in the Reich via the International Red Cross during the last three years are congesting warehouses here. The Geneva organization is unable to forward them because

> *no central Red Cross is permitted in Germany.* Other hundreds of tons are being held in New York pending a solution.
>
> "The contents of the packages tell a pitiful story," said Col. T. F. Wessels, provost marshall at U.S. army headquarters in Frankfurt, Germany, they contain chiefly wooden toys laboriously made by hand by the prisoners to send to their children, and even hand made shoes for their wives and mothers. Many German captives refrained from smoking and sent their cigarette alowances and candy. Many sent books about American life.[28]

An attempt is made by British officials to justify the enslavement on the grounds that the men are prisoners of war, and that as such they can be forced to work under the Geneva Convention rules. It is said that the war is not yet legally ended, that the prisoners are still soldiers of the German Government, and that when they return to Germany it will be the responsibility of the German Government to give them their pay accumulated as soldiers and prisoners. This argument rests on the assumption that there is a German government. But they also argue that repatriation of the prisoners cannot take place, as called for by the Geneva Convention as soon as hostilities are over, because there has been no armistice or peace treaty signed with Germany, and that none can be signed at present, because there is no German Government.

By similar double-talk they justify feeding the prisoners rations well below army standards on the pretext that the Geneva Convention which requires standard army rations has expired with World War II; yet, when press representatives ask to examine the prison camps, the British loudly refuse, with the excuse that the Geneva Convention bars such visits to prisoner-of-war camps.[29]

The International Red Cross, the highest authority on the subject, roundly condemns the slave system. As related from Geneva:

> The United States, Britain, and France, nearly a year after peace, are violating International Red Cross agreements they solemnly signed in 1929.
>
> Investigation at Geneva headquarters today disclosed that the transfer of German war prisoners captured by the American army to French and British authorities for forced labor is nowhere permitted in the statutes of the International Red Cross, which is the highest authority on the subject in the world.

Although thousands of the former German soldiers are being used in the hazardous work of clearing mine fields, sweeping sea mines, destroying surplus amunition and razing shattered buildings, the Geneva Convention expressly forbids employing prisoners "in any dangerous labor or in the transport of any material used in warfare."

Russia refused to attend the 1929 conference of the International Red Cross and Japan never ratified that convention, so neither Moscow nor Tokyo was bound by the provisions regulating war prisoners.

"The American delivery of German prisoners to the French and British for forced labor already is being cited by the Russians as justification for them to retain German army captives for as long as they are able to work," an International Red Cross official admitted. "The bartering of captured enemy soldiers by the victors throws the world back to the dark ages—when feudal barons raided adjoining duchies to replenish their human live stock."[30]

A Red Cross observer condemns the enslavement in these words:

> It is an iniquitous system and an evil precedent because it is wide open for abuses with difficulty in establishing responsibility. German soldiers were not common law convicts—they were drafted to fight in a national army on patriotic grounds and could not refuse military service any more than the Americans could. It is manifestly unjust to buy and sell them for political reasons as the African Negroes were a century ago.[31]

It must be emphasized, moreover, that many of the slaves were never German soldiers. Many were civilian Germans held in America during the war, including seamen picked up before we entered the war, former legal residents of the United States, and persons brought here by force from Latin America for having pro-German sentiments. Even anti-Nazi Germans who have voluntarily returned to Germany from America to help the military government rebuild the destroyed countries and to help families and friends in dire need have been nabbed for enslavement.[32]

In sharp contrast with our treatment of German war prisoners was German treatment of American war prisoners. Allan Wood, war front correspondent of the London *Express*, in summarizing German treatment of their prisoners said:

> The most amazing thing about the atrocities in this war is that there have been so few of them. I have come up against few

instances where the Germans have not treated prisoners according to the rules, and respected the Red Cross.[333]

Lieutenant Newton L. Marguiles, Assistant Judge Advocate of Jefferson Barracks, said in St. Louis, Mo., April 27, 1945:

> The Germans even in their greatest moments of despair obeyed the Convention in most respects. True it is that there were front line atrocities—passions run high up there—but they were incidents, not practices; and maladministration of their American prison camps was very uncommon.[34]

Chief of Staff Gen. George C. Marshall, on Jan. 5, 1945, wrote to the National Commander of the American Legion:

> Our treatment of them [prisoners of war] is governed by the Geneva convention which, among other provisions, requires them to be furnished rations equal in quality and quantity to those of American troops at base camps in this country. This is done as a matter of treaty obligation and our soldiers in German hands receive generally reciprocal treatment.[35]

The American Red Cross in 1945 reported officially that "99 per cent of the American prisoners of war in Germany have survived and are on their way home."

German treatment of Russian war prisoners was on a par with Russian treatment of German war prisoners. Since Russia had not signed the Geneva Convention, neither it nor Germany was bound by its provisions. And it must be remembered that the atrocities in German concentration camps did not involve war prisoners, but people supposed to be German, people who now proudly admit, those who have survived, that they were members of the German underground, saboteurs, doing their best to obstruct and defeat the German war effort. The treatment they received, while deplorable and inhuman in the extreme, is on a par with Russian treatment of her political prisoners. If one is to be condemned, so must the other, if there is to be justice. Otherwise, we are guilty of rank discrimination, condemning a crime committed by one, condoning or overlooking it when committed by another. If we really fought this war to stop such things, the war will not be over until the inmates of the Russian slave camps are also liberated. If we fought a half trillion dollar war to free those in German camps only, but not to free those in Russian camps, an explanation is due.

In any case, we must ask ourselves what we would do if we should go to war with, let us say, Russia, and were beset from within by an "underground" movement of sabotaging Communist fifth-columnists.

An attempt has been made to justify enslavement of the common man of Germany on the ground that the Nazi government exacted forced labor from foreign workers. It is true that the Reich had millions of imported workers, but it is also true that, except for special cases such as war prisoners coming under the Geneva Convention, they were for the most part paid and fed well.

Dr. James K. Pollock, for 14 months with AMG [American Military Government], said of Germany's "forced laborers": "I think some of the persons found themselves better off than at any time in their lives before."[36] A mass of evidence proves that this is true and that Allied war propaganda to the contrary was greatly exaggerated. Besides, there can be no justification for punishing the average citizen of any country for the sins of its political leaders.

In July, 1946, Max H. Forester, chief of AMG's coal and mining division when asked, "What did the Germans do to get efficient production for forced labor that we are not able to do with Germans working the mines?" replied: "They fed their help and fed them well."[37]

The American Federation of Labor in the summer of 1946 came out strongly against the slave system as a fundamental threat to free labor all over the world. Calling attention to tariff laws which specifically forbid the importation from foreign countries of goods produced wholly or in part by convict, forced, indentured, or any other form of involuntary labor,[38] AF of L spokesman Herbert Thatcher warned in a radio address that the slave labor system may grind down trade and production to a level that can lead to another war. Conditions of slave labor in Britain, France, and Russia, he said, "menace world peace and they destroy world trade." "Therefore, the American Federation of Labor," he concluded, "calls upon the United States government to propose to the United Nations that all member nations renounce the use of forced labor and agree to bar the products of forced labor from world trade."[39]

> We negotiated and concluded an agreement with the four dominant powers of the earth which for the first time made explicit and unambiguous what was theretofore, as the tribunal has declared, implicit in international law, namely, that . . . to enslave or deport civilian populations is an international crime and that for the commission of such crimes individuals are responsible.[40]

Willis Smith of Raleigh, N.C., President of the American Bar Association, in defending the Nuremberg convictions said:

> The time has come when men who order criminal things to be done should themselves be declared criminals. Since when are murder and deportations and slave labor not crimes?[41]

Denazification

Germany under Hitler was ruled by the single National Socialist German Workers party, with all other parties outlawed. The system in this respect was similar to that of the Communists of Russia who since the 1917 coup d'etat have enforced a one party system upon the Russian people and treated all dissident political opinions as treason.

Rejecting parliamentarienism, the Nazis followed what they called the leadership principle. The chief leader or "Führer" exercised supreme authority; under him descending layers of subordinate leaders spread out fan-wise through all branches of society to bring the entire German nation under centralized party control.

After it took over, leaders in all walks of life found it necessary or expedient to join the party or one or more of its affiliated organizations. Among its 7,500,000 members were nearly all government workers, professional men, scientists, technicians, professors, teachers, writers, and businessmen inducted as führers of business and compelled under heavy penalties, such as confiscation of property, to conform to party policies and mandates. White collar workers, craftsmen, and technicians had to fall in line to be eligible for promotion. Membership expanded rapidly during the war and the period of high tension immediately preceding. Party and nation became so closely identified that to join was to display patriotism; to refuse, to invite penalization for disloyalty. In short, almost everybody in Germany with brains, skills, and managerial ability belonged to the Nazi party, or one of its affiliated organizations and obeyed its orders.

join was to display patriotism; to refuse, to invite penalization for disloyalty. In short, almost everybody in Germany with brains, skills, and managerial ability belonged to the Nazi party, or one of its affiliated organizations and obeyed its orders.

By placing sole blame for the war on Germany and therefore the Nazi party, by declaring the war to be one of aggression, and by outlawing aggression as a crime against humanity, Germany's conquerors have condemned the Nazi party, its affiliates, and its millions of members as criminal. The punishment meted out at Potsdam, if carried out to the letter, would mean the virtual liquidation of Germany's middle and upper classes.

The blanket incrimination rests upon an infirm base, as revealed in the Potsdam denazification decrees. In one breath they order that all "discrimination on grounds of . . . political opinion shall be abolished"; yet in the next breath they permanently dissolve the Nazi party and its affiliated organizations and institutions, ban propagation of Nazi political opinion, without identifying it in particular, and call for severe punishment of all Nazis simply for being Nazis.

Potsdam commands that "Nazi leaders, influential Nazi supporters and high officials of Nazi organizations and institutions . . . shall be arrested and interned" and that all lesser Nazis "shall be removed from public and semi-public office and former positions of responsibility in private undertakings."

In attempting to carry out these unusual edicts, which were looked upon as a purge order "to throw the rascals out," the American military government issued "Law Number Eight" to denazify business and various mandatory removal edicts, the exact provisions of which were military secrets, to purge government of all Nazis. Approximately 3,000,000 German men were affected in our zone out of a total population of 16,682,000. Our occupation authorities jailed 75,000 and earmarked another 80,000 unreturned war prisoners for internment for being important Nazis; ousted more than 100,000 from public office; and denuded business of managerial and technical talent by firing and demoting hundreds of thousands of others.[42]

In other words, we set out to ruin the lives and reputations of three million men in our zone alone because, as they see it, they made a "political mistake." In consequence, the Germans are afraid to identify themselves with any political party or to express any political views, for fear of being punished later on, just as the Nazis are being punished now.

Most important of all, the zone and its people have been denied the economic benefits which would accrue if these men were permitted to do the work which they alone by talent, training, and experience are capable of performing. Putting the zone's most productive men in pick and shovel gangs and filling their places with incapables has been one of the chief contributing causes to the zone's economic paralysis.

Our occupation authorities have been confronted with two opposing mandates which often set them to working at cross purposes. They were ordered at Potsdam to secure enough production to supply the needs of the occupation forces and the "displaced persons," with enough left over "to enable the German people to subsist without external assistance." In the attempt to carry out this mandate some of our zonal authorities, for example, might be out scouring the zone with scanty success for trained personnel to run the undermanned railway system. But at the same time, some of our other authorities, attempting to enforce the denazification decrees, would be out ahead of the others nabbing and jailing trainmen and locomotive engineers, because they had been Nazis.

Administration of the denazification decrees proved to be a task of forbidding magnitude. The limited AMG personnel found it impossible to get the three million Nazis properly registered, their questionnaires filled out and tabulated, and proper files set up. Nor could individual trials and hearings for so many be properly conducted, especially when each error added to the rising tide of German indignation.

Fearing organized resistance, we carried out in Gestapo fashion one of the greatest mass raids in history. Striking at daybreak without warning, our troops halted every vehicle in our zone, checked the papers of civilians and soldiers, and swept through every German house from cellar to attic. Although the German populace had supposedly been under the influence and domination of criminals and criminal organizations for a dozen years, according to the men in charge "the search showed less crime than perhaps would be uncovered in a similar action over a comparable area in the United States."[49]

impossible to hold, yet difficult to drop. We therefore tossed it to the Germans for them to handle.

The law turning the job of denazification in our zone over to the Germans was largely formulated by one Heinrich Schmitt, a corpulent Communist Quisling serving under AMG as Bavarian Denazification Minister. The execution of the law was also partly placed in his hands.[44] This sort of thing is a logical outgrowth of the program which automatically places political responsibility on former political neutrals or active anti-Nazis, including Communists, who, with Communist Russia signing the Potsdam Declaration, must be accepted as "democratic."

The law is designed to permit some Nazis, otherwise condemned, to prove their innocence or pay the penalties and be restored to citizenship. It sets up five catgories of war criminals and potentially dangerous persons, namely:

1) Major offenders; 2) offenders broadly described as Nazi activists, militarists, and profiteers; 3) lesser offenders; 4) followers, constituting the broad membership of the party and affiliates; and 5) persons exonerated after a tribunal finds them innocent.

Penalties for those in the first category range from death or life imprisonment to imprisonment for five or more years with or without hard labor. Those in the second category may be imprisoned for a period up to ten years. Those in lower categories are subject to a variety of "sanctions," including loss of citizenship and the right to vote, debarment from public office, loss of personal rights such as the privilege to own an automobile, demotion in position with heavy cut in compensation, discharge from position, confiscation of property, and employment only at ordinary labor.[45]

To make matters easier, we granted an amnesty to all Nazis in our zone under 27 years of age who had no special charges against them. The action readmitted to citizenship about a million men who, as General Clay put it, had become Nazis before they were old enough to know what they were doing. He failed to explain why the same consideration might not apply to most of the older men as well. At any rate, the action was accompanied by a statement to the effect that it was the desire of the military government "to offer encourgement to the youth of Germany to understand and develop a democratic way of life."[46]

encouragement to the youth of Germany to understand and develop a democratic way of life."[46]

Unfortunately, most of those pardoned under the blanket order were in France, Britain, Belgium, Holland, Russia or elsewhere for indefinite terms performing forced labor in the manner of convicts.

Within a few months left-wing critics again began to complain that the elaborate German court system which had been set up to adjudicate the million remaining cases was far too lenient, that it was permitting Hitler's Hordes to creep back.* Nevertheless, in the autumn of 1946 the Allied Control Council's Coordinating Committee passed general denazification laws for the whole of Germany patterned after the American zonal law, with enforcement, however, left entirely to each zonal authority.[47] This loophole permits the other occupation governments to continue to denazify as they see fit, which thus far has been with greater reasonableness and leniency than have been exercised in the American zone where enforcement, in other words, has been far more rigid and drastic than elsewhere. At Stuttgart Mr. Byrnes was able to boast that denazification in the American zone had been completed.

Less than four weeks later, the Nuremberg tribunal handed down its momentous decision. Out of 22 arch-Nazis the Allied court, which certainly cannot be accused of judicial neutrality or leniency, and which tried the cases on four all-embracing counts, gave the death penalty to only 12, life imprisonment to three, prison terms ranging from 10 to 20 years to four, and acquitted three. If three of the very highest Nazis were free of all guilt, and four others were only partly guilty, the broad party membership could not be seriously guilty at all. This means that the denazification decrees which condemn all Nazis without trial are thoroughly unjust. The Nuremberg proceedings themselves have been roundly condemned for violating basic principles of Anglo-Saxon jurisprudence, particularly for condemning on the basis of ex

---

*In November 1946, Lt. Gen. Lucius D. Clay expressed concern over the leniency being shown Nazis in German courts. Setting a 60 day deadline before which the Germans must prove they had developed "the will to do this job which is not present today," he warned that the military government was ready to take back the job of denazification unless the German courts tightened up. The day before the following Christmas, Gen. McNarney proclaimed a general amnesty for approximately 800,000 "little Nazis" in the U.S. zone. Included were minor Nazis whose incomes during the calendar years 1943 and 1945 were less than 3,000 marks and whose taxable property in 1945 did not exceed 20,000 marks.

thoroughly unjust. The Nuremberg proceedings themselves have been roundly condemned for violating basic principles of Anglo-Saxon jurisprudence, particularly for condemning on the basis of ex post facto law, for placing partisan judges on the bench, and for excluding evidence that would reflect on the victorious powers. But the verdict handed down at Potsdam was still worse, for there a blanket verdict of guilty was pronounced, without even a pretense of trial, evidence, or testimony. Under the present denazification laws, all Nazis are still guilty, unless they can prove themselves innocent in the face of procedure which permits violation of the accepted rules of evidence.[48]

The Nuremberg tribunal also tried various Nazi organizations to determine whether or not they and their members were criminal. The SS, Gestapo, SD—elite guard, secret police, and security police—and the higher brackets of the Nazi leadership corps were adjudged criminal organizations. This means that for acquittal, some 400,000 members must prove they were forced to join or knew nothing of the criminality. Punishment ranges to the death penalty. On the other hand, the SA—original storm troopers—was dismissed as not linked with conspiracy to wage aggressive war, and the General Staff, High Command, and Brown Shirts were found not guilty. Certainly, then, the broad masses of the German people could not be guilty, and should not be punished.

The denazification program in general and the Nuremberg trial in particular violates our traditional ideas of justice; on the contrary, they embody the Nazi and Communist concept of jurisprudence—the liquidation of ideological opponents. As *Barron's* weekly says:

> . . . the punishment is being meted out one-sidedly to the vanquished. After all, except that they did not commit the same spectaular atrocities on the spot, the Russians did just about the same things in Poland that the Nazis did. Thus a combination of excusably fanatic Nazi-haters and purposeful fellow-travelers has provided a Roman holiday by exploiting our legitimate desire for a new international law. In the eyes of the world we have adopted the Communist view of justice.[49]

Even worse, we have permitted Communists, whose worst doctrines and those of the Nazis are identical, to continue to preach and agitate and even to work their way into key positions in our military government. When we first arrived the Germans were strongly anti-Communist; they have since started fleeing our zone and entering the Russian where they are welcomed into the Communist party and even into the Red Army, in whose ranks they may someday be able to get their revenge against us.

Denazification in the Russian zone has been far more enlightened and less economically disruptive. The strong men of the Kremlin could hardly take seriously the condemnation of all Nazis as criminals when they know full well that their own party, which rules Russia much as the Nazi party ruled Germany and which demands the same blind obedience of its members, is guilty of every act for which we so strongly condemn the Nazis: wars of aggression against peaceful neighbors, wars of nerves, confiscation of property of whole classes without compensation to the owners, violation of treaties and agreements, hostility toward religion, concentration camp atrocities, slave labor, looting and abusing conquered countries, the use of fifth columns and Quislings, one-party rule by terror with the aid of civilian informers and a brutal secret police system, stifling of human rights and individual liberties of all kinds, and even the aim to conquer the world.

The Russians know this and so do the Germans. When we condone the one and condemn the other we become ridiculous in the eyes of both.

The attitude of the Kremlin toward denazification was expressed years ago and probably has not changed since. Russia in partnership with Hitler had just attacked, defeated, and partitioned Poland and Hitler had proposed that since the issue which had started the war had been settled, all the belligerents should stop fighting and call a general disarmament conference. Britain and France had declined with the terse remark that they would fight on for the "extermination of Hitlerism." The Kremlin scoffed. Its reaction, which is probably still its inner conviction, was reported by the Associated Press from highly censored Moscow (Oct. 9, 1939), as follows:

> Soviet Russia threw her weight behind Adolph Hitler's peace gestures today in an editorial in the government newspaper *Izvestia*, accusing Great Britain and France of "returning to the middle ages" for waging war to "exterminate Hitlerism."

> *Izvestia* asserted British-French arguments that the war must be prolonged to crush Hitlerism "makes us return to the gloomy middle ages when devastating religious wars were carried on to exterminate heretics and people of different religions." The paper asserted:
>
> "It is impossible to exterminate any idea or any opinion by fire and sword.
>
> "One may respect or hate Hitlerism or any other system of political opinion. That is a matter of taste. But to begin a war for the 'extermination of Hitlerism' means to admit to criminal silliness in policy."

Potsdam's decrees calling for the "extermination of Hitlerism" have been highly useful to the Kremlin, however, for they have provided a basis for the liquidation of the German "bourgeoisie" and therefore set the stage for ultimate communization. The necessary expropriation of property has been accomplished through confiscation of the holdings of Nazis, absentee fugitives, "war profiteers," and other classes of synthetic criminals. But once a nominal Nazi in the Russian zone has been dispossessed he is offered a chance to redeem himself. He is given his job back if he works satisfactorily for six months with clean-up crews. Denazification is thus linked to "aufbau" or reconstruction.[50] Minor offenders have been tried in German courts and penitent Nazis are invited to join the Communist party.[51] According to Reuters, German military officers have been taken into the Red army by invitation. When the officers cross the zonal frontiers they are nominally "arrested," placed in quarantine camps, and invited to enlist. Upon acceptance, they are given preferential treatment. In other words, the union of the Red and Nazi armies has begun.[52]

In her zone, Russia is taking full advantage of the many points of similarity between her own system and that of the Nazis under Hitler. Some Germans are remarking that "Communism is nothing but National Socialism under a different name."[53] While we continue to pound away at the evils of Nazism, which we apparently consider as something unique, Russia, which our army men have been ordered not to criticize, matches up these evils to those of her own system and thereby facilitates the desired transformation from the one to the other.

By eliminating the "bourgeoisie" in our zone we have played into the Kremlin's hands, for the action has removed the principle barrier to the establishment of the "dictatorship of the proletariat," and ultimate absorption of the zone into the Soviet Union—the Kremlin's own United Nations. Our entire denazification procedure has been highly satisfactory to Moscow, for the greater the chaos, despair, and disgust we create, and the greater the resentment of the German people becomes, the stronger becomes the grip of Communism, and the closer we come to losing everything for which we fought the war.

CHAPTER FOUR

The Attack Against German Capital

Looting

The sacking of Germany after her unconditional surrender will go down in history as one of the most monstrous acts of modern times. Its excess beggars description and its magnitude defies condemnation.

Allied armies that swept into Germany came with blood in their eyes and the conviction born of propaganda that the Germans had lost caste as members of the human race, were unworthy of protection afforded by human law and civilized institutions such as property rights and security of person. It was not thought of as looting, but simply as helping one's self to property the Germans had forfeited by being German.

Russian soldiers were particularly ravenous, their appetites for loot being restrained only by the limitation placed on their own rights to hold property. Things the individual Russian soldier could keep, such as wrist watches, they snatched on sight, even from the arms of Yankees.

The serious looting by the Russians was conducted officially, systematically and thoroughly. Every house and apartment was entered, searched, and stripped of every thing at once valuable and movable—jewelry, silverware, works of art, clothing, household appliances, money. Stores, shops, warehouses were ransacked. Farms were denuded of farm animals, machinery, seed reserves, fodder, wine and food stocks. Telephones were removed from residences, telephone and telegraph lines and equipment were dismantled. Automobiles, motor trucks, even fire engines, were seized. Everything not nailed down was hauled away.[1] For the

the German standard of living must be lowered to the average of Europe.

The Russian armies of occupation, kept equal in size to the combined occupation forces of the western powers, live off the land, paying for requisitions by paper occupation marks. Exorbitant occupation costs afford the Kremlin an effective device for milking the territory. Charges in the Soviet zone of Austria are several times greater, relatively, than those the Germans imposed on France, Belgium, Holland, Greece, and elsewhere.[2] This, despite Austria's promised "liberated" status.

All of the Allies have issued huge amounts of military currency which the Germans are forced to accept in "payment." It is conservatively estimated that altogether they have pumped into the country between 15 billion and 20 billion occupation marks as against a normal currency circulation of between 7 and 9 billion.[3] This means that the four powers have obtained between 2 and 4 billion dollars' worth of German property for the mere cost of printing money issued in payment.

* * * * *

Just as there was a preponderance of American forces in the armies that struck against the west and south of Germany, so in these sectors was the preponderance of the looting American. *Chicago Daily News* foreign correspondent William H. Stoneman, stationed with the U.S. 3rd Army, wrote in May, 1945, when Germany was surrendering:

> I have been impressed by the careless manner in which the booty has been handled and the way in which great stocks of foodstuffs have been left to the reckless inroads of looters.[4]

A few days later he cabled:

> Millions of dollars worth of rare things varying from intricate Zeiss lenses to butter and cheese and costly automobiles are being destroyed because the Army has not organized a system for the recovery of valuable enemy material.
>
> Frontline troops are rough and ready about enemy property. They naturally take what they find if it looks interesting, and, because they are in the front lines, nobody says anything.
>
> There are no M.P.s in the front lines.

But what front-line troops take is nothing compared to the damage caused by wanton vandalism of some of the following troops.

> They seem to ruin everything, including the simplest personal belongings of the people in whose houses they are billeted.
>
> Today, we have had two more examples of this business, which would bring tears to the eyes of anybody who has appreciation of material values.
>
> First I found two boxcars loaded with magnificent Zeiss range-finders for ack-ack guns, thousands of rare lenses, worth at rough estimate, perhaps $1,000,000.
>
> Most of the things we saw there—many of them scattered about the tracks—were priceless, and thousands of dollars worth of stuff had been scattered as G.I.s combed boxcars for binoculars and other items which appeared easy to sell. Anybody with any knowledge of precision instruments would have cried his eyes out to see instruments worth $500 to $1,000 scattered around like so much junk.
>
> Later I visited a warehouse which had been loaded with textiles and it was like a pigsty.
>
> There still were thousands of yards of printed cotton goods and artificial woolen goods lying around, but much more had been looted by somebody or other.[5]

In one case looting resulted in arrests and trials. A WAC Captain and a Colonel were arrested in America and tried in Frankfurt, Germany, for taking $1,500,000 worth of jewels, mostly of the House of Hesse, from a castle owned by Princess Margaret of Hesse, granddaughter of Queen Victoria. Defense attorneys at the trials made clear the extent of looting which had been done and the philosophy behind it. An on the scene account reads as follows:

> The princess scored heavily against the defense contention that the owners of the jewels were *just a bunch of Nazis* whose loss was a misfortune of war which should not be singled out for prosecution from among *hundreds of thousands of thefts from Germans* by the American army personnel.[6] (emphasis added)

It is, indeed, unlikely that the case would have gone to trial had the owners lacked such imposing connections. It is well known that we took from German museums some 200 art masterpieces with the intention of keeping them. Public opinion was so outraged that President Truman found it expedient to promise their return; yet no one was prosecuted or even arrested.

American Provost Marshall Lt. Col. Gerald F. Beane, whose duty it is to deal with crimes committed by our soldiers, in an official report released in Berlin late in 1945 on the nature and extent of criminality in our army of occupation stated that larceny and robbery are the crimes most frequently committed by our soldiers. A leading daily comments:

> As to the crimes against property, the explanation is fairly obvious. No effective steps were taken to discourage looting by the invading armies during the war. Officers and men alike committed this crime and for much the most part went unpunished. It was tolerated under some such euphemism as souvenir collecting. The habit of stealing, once formed, is difficult to break. The fault, of course, lies with the high command which permitted the abuse. Col. Beane's pronouncement suggests that the army is tardily seeking to correct its error.[7]

Most of this type of looting died out during the first year of occupation; after that the methods became more subtle and indirect. Late in July, 1946, GI's were called to task for "sleeper purchases" of German properties which could be bought at the time for almost nothing, but which may some day have great value.[8] Full advantage has been taken of the currency chaos. In September, 1946, military authorities, to kill American profiteering in the black markets and illegal acquisition of foreign exchange, issued a new scrip currency, to replace all "foreign and allied military currencies in financial transactions throughout United States army installations."[8] And if official Russian accusations can be given credence, American officials have stolen equipment from plants in our zone earmarked for shipment to Russia on reparations account and sold it to foreign countries for their personal profit.[10]

However, the type of looting just discussed, although it has run in value into hundreds of millions of dollars and robbed the German people of comforts and necessities they have sorely needed during the dreadful days through which they are having to pass, is but petty larceny as compared to the gigantic program of industrial sacking authorized at Potsdam.

Economic Cannibalism

Potsdam decrees that future German production shall be so limited by the Allied Control Council that the average German standard of living will not exceed the average of the standards of living of other European countries, exclusive of Britain and Russia, and that "productive capacity not needed for permitted production" shall be taken by the conquerors as plunder or destroyed. The prostrated German economy must be drawn and quartered and its flesh fed to other economies, a project which has aptly been called "economic cannibalism."

Potsdam piously recites, as a mere observation, not a mandate, that the program "should leave enough resources to enable the German people to subsist without external assistance." At the same time it admits that remaining resources are disastrously inadequate, for it says that the war and defeat "have destroyed German economy and made chaos and suffering inevitable." Still, it proceeds to lay down a reparations program to destroy or remove a large part of the scanty remaining production facilities.

After much wrangling and horse trading, the Control Council in March, 1946, reached its decisions fixing the future levels of production both for Germany as a whole and for individual industries in accordance with Potsdam's stipulations. As a top limit, but by no means a guaranteed minimum, Germany's output under these orders may reach by 1949, but not surpass, the level to which it plunged at the bottom of the great depression of 1932, just before the Nazis were voted into power, when a third of the German workers were unemployed.

In carrying out the Potsdam mandate calling for the "elimination or control of all German industry that could be used for military production" and emphasis on "the development of agriculture and peaceful domestic industries," many ordinarily peaceful industries are entirely prohibited. These include shipbuilding, manufacture and operation of airplanes, ball and taper roller bearings, nearly all types of heavy machine tools, heavy materials, aluminum, magnesium, beryllium, vanadium, radioactive materials, hydrogen peroxide, and synthetic oil, gasoline and ammonia.

Exports and imports are rigidly controlled and drastically restricted. Payments for necessary imports are given first call on proceeds from exports. Imports are confined mostly to a small amount of food and nitrates for fertilizer; exports are limited largely to coal, potash, and lumber. Foreign trade in the ordinary sense has been impossible, however, and will remain so, as long as the mark is given no value in terms of other currencies.

Future production of a large number of domestic industries is drastically restricted. Electrical engineering is cut in half;

mechanical engineering by two-thirds. Synthetic textiles are sharply curtailed. Over-all chemical production is reduced to 45 per cent of the old level. Steel production may not surpass 5,800,000 ingot tons a year, against the former 54,000,000[10A] ton capacity. Britain had argued that such a level would turn the Reich into an economic desert and had fought for a 7,500,000 ton level. Since Russia had held out for a much lower figure, however, the 5,800,000 ton ceiling was reached as a compromise.

All during the negotiations Russia had fought for extremely low production ceilings. She had even asked for a sharp reduction in permitted food imports, to reduce the volume of necessary exports, and thus to free more industrial booty in which she was to share. When a little later shipment of reparations to her from the western zones was halted, she suddenly reversed her stand, however, and asked for higher ceilings. Molotov specifically demanded higher coal production and said, "The Reich must be permitted more steel, greater industry and foreign trade."

Mr. Byrnes at Stuttgart stubbornly defended the agreed production ceilings and insisted the program would permit some betterment in the German standard of living if the German people would work and save hard enough.

Apart from generating bitter despair through closing the door to any hope of achieving prosperity, the ceilings have had little practical significance, because actual German output has remained far below the permitted levels. Our military authorities have asserted that it will require years for German recovery to reach the ceilings which have been set. The current effect of the program has been largely confined to repression of power to produce thorough destruction and removal of productive capacity and other measures, such as the banning of scientific research.

German science, upon which German industry depended heavily, has been dealt a lethal blow, partly by direct prohibitions and partly by the operations of the denazification decrees which automatically ended the careers of the great majority of German scientists, at least within the Reich. Potsdam has ordered control of "all German public or private scientific bodies, research and experimental institutions, laboratories, etc., connected with economic activities." In harmony with this decree, German science has been suppressed by orders from the Control Council.

Research (in Germany) by scientists who had been Nazis or had contributed to the development of German weapons, secret or otherwise, has been banned. Others, and they are very few, are forbidden to probe into a long list of specific, comprehensive subjects, 10 general categories of chemicals, and anything of military value or nature. Pure or theoretical science – explorations into the basic laws of nature and the like – may be conducted by the few eligibles, but only under military government surveillance.

In other words, German science has been destroyed, and with it German ability to compete commercially with the war victors.

German scientists, as a matter of fact, have become a highly esteemed form of war plunder. Russia, the first to recognize their value, was unable to hide her anxiety and frantic efforts to grab as many as she could. Britain, France, and the United States were not slow in following her example, entering the competition with marked success. We even managed to kidnap a large number from the western Russian zone when we retired to let the Russians take over. At first our interest was confined to experts who had been working on war developments, especially atomic fission and secret weapons. Others in our zone, including numbers who had fled before the Red armies, were held in jail. We changed this wasteful policy, however, after Dr. Roger Adams, head of the chemistry department of the University of Illinois and scientific adviser to the deputy governor of AMG, declared it unwise to confine ourselves only to war industry scientists, since many of those languishing in prison would prove equally valuable to us for other purposes if we chose to use them. In consequence we have now at our disposal hundreds of ex-German scientists who no doubt constitute one of our most profitable acquisitions taken from the fallen Reich. Perhaps they should be counted as reparation.

In addition we have sent into Germany teams of experts to scour the country and search out all German patents, designs, and secret processes, privately owned, or otherwise. According to Assistant Secretary of State William L. Clayton, in testimony before a U.S. Senate committee in June 1945:

> We intend to secure the full disclosure of all existing German technology and invention for the benefit of the United Nations . . . This Government and other governments with which Germany has been at war have reduced to their control inventions and designs

> both patented and unpatented which were owned and controlled by German nationals at the time of the outbreak of war . . . It is probable that no steps will be taken by either the legislative or executive branch of this government which would have the effect of returning such rights to the former German owners.

Mr. Morgenthau called for the industrial sacking of Germany by proposing that, instead of repeating the mistake made after the last war by demanding "reparations in the form of *future payments and deliveries*," requiring production and sale of exports, this time:

> . . . reparations shall be effected by the transfer of *existing resources and territories*, e.g. . . . by transfer of German territory and *German private rights* in industrial property situated in such territory to invaded countries . . .; by the removal and distribution among devastated countries of industrial plants and equipment . . .; by forced German labor outside Germany; and by confiscation of *all German Assets of any character whatsoever* outside of Germany. (emphasis added)

These proposals to trample on the sanctity of private German property could hardly fail to meet with wholehearted approval in the Politburo. In effecting the program no pretense is made that the owners of confiscated private property will be compensated now or later by either the Allies or the German government, for the latter, if it is ever established, will no doubt be so weak that such compensation would be beyond its financial capacity.

Yet the Hague convention in Article 46 in the section dealing with "Military Authority Over the Territory of the Hostile State" says: "*Private property cannot be confiscated.*" Article 53 underscores the point by saying that any private property taken during an occupation "must be restored and compensation fixed when peace is made."

In view of the present deadly, worldwide assault against the institution of private property, those who pretend to be its defenders should insist upon adherence to these provisions of international law. Flagrant Big Four violations not only create the injustices the laws were established to prevent but incriminate the victors of World War II for the very actions for which they so strongly and justly condemned Hitler. One can readily understand why Socialistic Soviet Russia would violate private property rights in occupied countries, but the same cannot be said of the United States.

Russia at Yalta took the lead in demanding that German reparations be set at 20 billion dollars, half of which was to go to herself. President Roosevelt, engrossed as he was in his "great design," gambling that Russian suspicions of the western capitalistic powers could be allayed by giving Stalin everything he wanted, and more, agreed to support the demand. Prime Minister Churchill, however, pointed out the obvious fact that if Germany was to be so weakened by de-industrialization that she could not pay reparations from current production and if reparation was to be limited to plant and equipment discarded by de-industrialization, there could be no justification for Russia's position. The de-industrialization program would automatically limit the amount of reparation to the amount to plant and equipment not ruined by war, less whatever amount would be left to the Germans. For the sake of harmony, however, the 10 billion dollar figure was accepted "as a basis for discussion."

At Potsdam Russia was apportioned the lion's share of the reparation. She was to receive all from her own zone, plus 25 per cent from the other zones. Of the latter, two-fifths was to go to Russia outright and three-fifths was to be given to her "in exchange for an equivalent value of food, coal, potash, zinc, timber, clay products, petroleum products, and such other commodities as may be agreed upon," presumably to be taken from her zone. President Truman said of the arrangement: "It is a means of maintaining a balanced economy in Germany and providing the usual exchange of goods between the eastern part and the western." In other words, one section of German economy must give up to Russia 15 per cent of the flesh to be stripped from its bones in order to receive sustenance from another section—a most remarkable form of economic cannibalism.

The value of Germany's bombed and battered plant and equipment remaining at the end of the war has been officially estimated at between 5 and 10 billion dollars, of which 45 per cent was located in the Russian zone where Russia was given a free hand. Under the "level of industry plan" 40 per cent of this was to be available for removal as reparation or destroyed. Total reparation, therefore, could not be more than 2 to 4 billions, and if Russia were to adhere to the general plan in her zone her total share from all Germany could not exceed 2.4 billion dollars.

At first Russia went along amicably with the program and, according to some reports, apparently took far less than the 40 per cent allowable from her own zone. In March, 1946, the head of the local Thuringian government told correspondents permitted to visit there on a conducted tour that Russia has dismantled less than 100 out of Thuringia's 5,200 industries.[10] A later report had it that out of 6,272 industries in the province only 310 had been dismantled, of which 80 had been able to get under way again.[12] Neither gave the relative size of the establishments seized. If the plants taken were of average size, they constituted only 2 to 5 per cent of the total. Early in the summer of 1946 the United States estimated that actual removals from the Russian zone amounted to between 500 and 750 million dollars, exclusive of war booty, restitution for destroyed or stolen Russian goods, or occupation costs.[13] This was still less than the allowance. Considering how thoroughly she stripped such regions as Manchuria and northern Iran before evacuating her troops, her early restraint in her German zone, if true, would suggest an ulterior motive.

What this motive might be is indicated by the fact, also according to reports, that over 90 per cent of the plants in her zone were in operation, with from 80 to 100 per cent of their output going to Russia as occupation costs or reparation. For example, at one plant with an output of 20 million razors, the German market was to receive 3 million; the rest was to go to the Soviet Union. Persistent rumors, moreover, told of large German munitions plants operating day and night in the zone producing munitions and implements of war for the Soviet Union.

Meanwhile reparations shipments from the western zones had gotten under way in April. The first shipment was six shiploads carrying the physical assets of the Deschimag shipyard, Germany's largest, valued at $4,800,000. Soon to follow were 20 carloads of machinery and tools valued at $5,000,000, representing half of the assets of the country's largest ball bearing plant. Other early shipments included the Gendorf unit of the Anorgana Chemical works, valued at $10,000,000 and the vast Daimler-Benz underground aircraft engine plant near Oberingheim.

By May, according to Reparations Commissioner Edwin W. Pauley, the U.S. zone had earmarked 144 plants for removal to Russia, of which 35 or 40 were actually shipped, before we suddenly halted further shipments on the ground that we must do so to protect the economic interests of our zone until interzonal economic unity had been achieved, in harmony with Potsdam. Shortly before this, however, the western powers had failed to get the Russians to agree on how much inspection a four power commission would be allowed to do in all four zones, including the Russian. The idea has originated in the Paris conference of Foreign Ministers to allay interzonal suspicions and to give each occupying power a clearcut picture of disarmament in other zones. Britain has hinted that she wanted to check rumors that munitions were being turned out in the Russian zone; Russia had retorted with the direct accusation that Britain had not disbanded large units of the captured German army and wanted to investigate.

Whatever the reasons, we stopped further shipments of reparations from our zone. And then the storm broke loose.

Russia apparently reversed her whole attitude toward Germany. In June at Paris Molotov declared it ridiculous to try to destroy Germany, called for a strong, centralized and economically balanced Reich with the Ruhr and Saar attached, specifically asked for higher steel and coal production levels than those Russia had previously agreed upon, saying, "The Reich must be permitted more steel, greater industry and foreign trade," and added, "The Soviet Government insists that reparations from Germany to the amount of ten billion dollars be exacted without fail." His object was clear: Russia now wanted a Germany able and required to pay large reparations so heavy that socialization would become mandatory, with anschluss with the Union of Socialist Soviet Republics to follow.

Meanwhile, Russia was stripping her zone to the bone, implying that it was necessary to do so to guarantee a continued flow of reparations to the Soviet Union. Many of Germany's greatest producers of civilian goods were dismantled and shipped eastward. Among them were the two largest shoe factories (Lingel and Tack); the largest sugar refineries in the great beet-sugar region; the largest grain processing mills in Europe, at Barby near Magdeburg; the great Bemberg Silk Mills, famous before the war for their hosiery and lingerie, and the Zeiss Optical Works at Jena. All secondary rail lines were torn up and all electric locomotives removed from the zone.

But many of the confiscated plants were left in Germany where they could be operated by Germans for Russia's benefit. She installed Russian or Communist foremen and placed Russians or Communists on the Boards of Directors. In this fashion she acquired complete ownership and control of 200 of Germany's key industries comprising the zone's real economic wealth and employing 1,300,000 workers—a third of the zone's working population. Examples of the industries seized are all of the I.G. Farben Industrie plants in Saxony, including the famous Leuna chemical factories at Merseburg, Bitterfeld, and Wollin; the Reich's only important copper works, the Mansfield Co., in Saxony; the machine works of Krupp-Gruson at Magdeburg; the Brabag Brown Coal and Gasoline Co., near Gera in Thuringia; the Polysius machine works at Dessau; and many of the most important iron ore plants, machine tool factories, coal mine companies, potash mines, and electrical plants.

America, which from the beginning had been the most zealous in carrying out de-industrialization in its own zone, made no protest to Russia until it was learned that two establishments owned by American concerns, the United Shoe Machinery Co. and the Corn Products Refining Co., had been among those seized. We then offered the suggestion that Allied-owned property should be exempted from seizure and added the pious thought that plants producing civilian goods should be kept in Germany. Our note went unanswered. It is known, however, that Russia has invented numerous excuses to give her seizures apparent legality, among them being the contention that plants with international backing are abandoned property and that the owners, most of whom have fled or been liquidated, were war profiteers.

Since Britain had come forward with a scheme to nationalize the Ruhr and other industries in her zone, potentially worth billions of dollars, in a manner that would place title to much of it in her own hands as "custodian" without one cent of compensation to the former owners, she had lost all moral ground on which to base a protest against the Russian action. Nor could the French object, in view of their avaricious, vengeful treatment of their own zone, where looting has been just as thorough as in the Russian, but far less intelligent; where, for example, they demand most of the crops to be harvested and at the same time requisition draft animals in July just when most needed to help gather the harvest.

Although America went about the business of dismantling and dynamiting German plants with more fervor than was at first exhibited in any other zone, our motive was quite different from the motives of our allies. Russia is anxious to get as much loot as possible from Germany and yet to make it produce abundantly for Russia to help make her new five year plan successful, and ultimately to abosrb the Reich into the Soviet Union. France is ravenous for loot, has been anxious to destroy Germany forever and to annex as much of her territory as possible. Britain has found uses for large amounts of German booty, wants to get rid of Germany as a trade competitor, while retaining her as a market for British goods. The United States has no use for German plant and equipment as booty, and has often said so. We consider our own abundant production equipment superior. Apart from one or two special cases, our primary interest in German assets has been in those located outside Germany, to eliminate German competition in world trade. We are willing to permit the German people to subsist on their own little plot of land, if they can, but we are determined that they never again shall engage in foreign commerce on an important scale. In partnership with Britain we have carried out a systematic campaign to root out all German contacts and assets located abroad and have put our own traders in their place.

Known as the "replacement program," the campaign is closely related to the "safehaven" program which calls for the forcible elimination of all accumulations of German capital abroad.

The following extracts from testimony by assistant Secretary of State William L. Clayton before the "Kilgore Committee" of the U.S. Senate, June 25, 1945, tell the story:

LATIN AMERICA

> The government soon determined that German enterprises could not be permitted to survive . . . in this hemisphere. The replacement program was accordingly evolved as a means of bringing about the elimination of German enterprises and of German interests.
>
> The businesses of any persons who were acting against the political and economic independence or security of the American republics "shall be the object of forced transfer or total liquidation." German economic and political penetration in this hemisphere has, for the most part, been dealt a blow from which it will probably not recover . . .

THE SAFEHAVEN PROGRAM

> The replacement and safehaven programs are both based upon the common knowledge that totalitarian Germany was able to marshall the ostensible private interests of German nationals abroad for the purpose of waging economic war. The safehaven program concerns itself with denying to Germany among other things the German capital investments already located abroad when the war began. The financial and corporate interests of German nationals located outside of Germany have either been seized or will be subject to seizure. (Mr. Clayton also advocated that Germans with brains and skills, including citizens of Latin American countries of German extraction who had publicly expressed any sympathy for the German cause, should be extradited and sent to Germany.)

Accordingly, we have confiscated nearly a billion dollars of property in this country believed by our Justice Department to be owned by Germans, although held in the name of citizens of neutral countries such as Sweden and Switzerland. Attorney General Clark says the Justice Department contends these holdings now belong to the United States Government.

The external operation of the program has been illustrated by our forcing Switzerland, Sweden, Spain and other countries to hand over their German owned assets. Sweden, for example, held German wealth valued at 104 million dollars. At the same time we held 200 million dollars of Swedish assets which we had "blocked," that is, cut off from Swedish control during the war. We used these blocked funds as a club to compel Sweden to turn the assets over to us. After long negotiations, she finally did deliver 77 million dollars worth of the German resources and we in turn unblocked the 200 million dollars in Swedish funds in America. After obtaining the funds we confiscated them and divided the loot with Britain and France.

We were able to obtain half of the 200 to 250 million dollars worth of German assets held in Switzerland and pried loose over 100 million dollars worth of German assets from Spain. We have used and are using every weapon and pressure at our command to root out and confiscate German assets all over the world, and in the process, as Mr. Clayton testified, have dealt a death blow to German foreign trade.

That we officially recognize that the program will also destroy Germany and exterminate the German people was made perfectly clear by Mr. Clayton in his testimony before the Kilgore Committee. Dr. Schimmel, chief investigator, had inquired of the Under-Secretary of State if it were not true that the Germans had made their successful penetration of South American trade for the purpose of acquiring superior information facilities. Mr. Clayton replied:

> With the Germans it was not a matter of information, it was largely a matter of necessity. I mean *they had to have foreign trade, they had to export in order to live*. The country has, as you know, very little natural resources. The only natural resources of any consequence that they have are coal and potash, and they had to export manufactured goods in order to acquire the raw materials that they needed in their economic life, in their industry, and *foreign trade was an absolute necessity for the Germans*. (emphasis added)

Taking their foreign trade away from them, and making it impossible for them to export manufactured goods, the program advocated by Mr. Clayton and embodied in the Potsdam agreements, was tantamount, therefore, to pronouncing the death sentence on the German people.

CHAPTER FIVE

Bastardizing the German Race

Not only have the conquerors set out to destroy Germany economically by pulling down the three pillars of production but they have launched an assault against the German race itself by an attack against its mothers. From the record it appears that the men who met at Yalta deliberately formulated a diabolical program of racial bastardization which they considered an appropriate response to the claim of racial superiority.

A Russian General told General Ira Eaker, Commander of the Mediterannean air forces: "We've decided just to kill all the German men, take 17,000,000 German women and that will solve it." Something on this order was obviously the intent. The millions of German men of marriageable age not killed or disabled in war were marched off into slavery where they could not protect their wives, sweethearts, daughters and sisters. And then the attack began.

From the east came the Bolshevized Mongolian and Slavic hordes, repeatedly raping every captured woman and girl, contaminating them with venereal diseases and impregnating them with a future race of Russo-German bastards. In the west the British used colonial troops, the French Sengalese and Moroccans, the Americans an excessively high percentage of negroes. Our own method was not so direct as the Russian: instead of using physical force, we compelled the German women to yield their virtue in order to live – to get food to eat, beds to sleep in, soap to bathe with, roofs to shelter them.

Senator Eastland of Mississippi, after a European tour of observation, told his colleagues in the U.S. Senate early in December, 1945: "The virtue of womanhood and the value of human life are civilized man's most sacred possessions, yet they are the very cheapest thing in Russian-occupied Germany today."

He had learned first-hand of such incidents as the following, told by a priest in a letter smuggled out of Breslau, Germany, September 3, 1945:

> In unending succession were girls, women and nuns violated . . . Not merely in secret, in hidden corners, but in the sight of everybody, even in churches, in the streets and in public places were nuns, women and even eight-year-old girls attacked again and again. Mothers were violated before the eyes of their children; girls in the presence of their brothers; nuns, in the sight of pupils, were outraged again and again to their very death and even as corpses.[1]

Meanwhile newspaper headlines assured us that "Ivan and Joe Are Brothers Under the Skin."

Prime Minister Churchill had told the Germans in January, 1945, just before they surrendered unconditionally:

> We Allies are no monsters. This, at least, I can say on behalf of the United Nations . . . Peace, though based on unconditional surrender, will bring to Germany and Japan immense and immediate alleviation of suffering and agony.[2]

When our Russian Allies "liberated" Danzig they promptly liberated all the women of their virtue and chastity—by raping all—from small girls to ladies as much as 83 years of age. A 50-year-old teacher says that her niece, 15, was violated seven times the day after the Russians arrived, while her other niece, 22, was raped 15 times the same day. When women of the city pleaded for protection, a Russian officer told them to seek shelter in the Catholic Cathedral. After hundreds of women and girls were securely inside, the brave sons of mother Russia entered and "playing the organ and ringing the bells, kept up a foul orgy through the night, raping all the women, some more than 30 times.[3]

A Catholic pastor of Danzig states: "They even violated eight-year-old girls and shot boys who tried to shield their mothers."

It was the same in all regions overrun by the Communist Armies. When Berlin fell the Commander told his Russian soldiers the women of the city were theirs, to help themselves. They did! The only escape the women had was suicide.

The following is an eye-witness account of what the Russians did in eastern Germany written by a veteran American newspaperman who had been taken prisoner by the Germans in Paris and later freed by the Russians with whom he stayed for nearly three months as they swept over eastern Germany and on to Berlin and beyond:

> REDS TERRORIZE CONQUERED WITH RAPE AND DEATH
>
> London, August 4, 1945—As our long line of British Army lories (trucks) carrying American, British, and French liberated prisoners of war from the Russian to the main Anglo-American zone of Germany rolled through the main street of Brahlstorf, the last Russian occupied-town, a pretty blond girl darted from the crowd of Germans watching us and made a dash for our truck.
>
> Clinging with both hands to the tailboard, she made a desperate effort to climb in. But we were driving too fast and the board was too high. After being dragged several hundred yards she had to let go and fell on the cobblestone street.
>
> That scene was a dramatic illustration of the state of terror in which women in Russian-occupied eastern Germany were living. All these women, Germans, Polish, Jewish, and even Russian girls "freed" from Nazi slave camps were dominated by one desperate desire—to escape from the Red zone.
>
> In the district around our internment camp—the territory comprising the towns of Schlawe, Lauenburg, and Buckow and hundreds of larger villages—*Red soldiers during the first weeks of their occupation raped every woman and girl between the ages of 12 and 60. That sounds exaggerated but it is the simple truth.* (emphasis added)
>
> The only exceptions were girls who managed to remain in hiding in the woods or who had the presence of mind to feign illness—typhoid, dyptheria or some other infectious disease. Flushed with victory—and often with wine found in the cellars of rich Pomeranian land owners—the Reds searched every house for women, cowing them with pistols or tommy guns, and carried them into their tanks or trucks.
>
> Husbands and fathers who attempted to protect their women folk were shot down and girls offering extreme resistance were murdered.
>
> Some weeks after the invasion, Red "political commissions" began a tour of the countryside ostensibly in search of members of the Nazi party. In every village the woman were told to report for

examination of papers to these commissions, which looked them over and detained those with sex appeal. The youngest and prettiest were taken by the officers and the rest left to the mercy of the privates.

This reign of terror lasted as long as I was with the Reds in Pomerania. Several girls whom I had known during my captivity committed suicide. Others died after having been raped by ten soldiers in succession.

In an isolated farmhouse where my French comrade and myself spent three months after joining the Reds, there were eight young girls from neighboring villages hiding from the Reds. One was always on watch and when the Russians were seen approaching they scampered off into a nearby woods and hid in the dense underbrush. This sometimes happened several times daily and the girls never had a quiet moment but while we were there the Reds never discovered them.

All of these girls already had been raped and three of them—one a little girl of 13—were pregnant.

Inevitably the Red occupation is having a disastrous effect on the morality of the inhabitants and the existing conditions of anarchy will exert an evil influence for years. Many woman have been infected with venereal diseases and now a very few youthful girls have joined the Reds for pleasure and food and are helping them spot their compatriots.

Whenever possible, girls attach themselves to liberated Anglo-American or French prisoners of war for protection against the Russians. Curiously, the Reds seemed to have a special code of honor in this respect—they will take an Allied prisoner's watch but won't touch his girl.

When the Red Army starts a big offensive its commanders held out prospects of unrestricted rape and pillage as encouragement to the troops, but later they try to stem the tide of lust—not on grounds of humanity but because it threatens to undermine discipline.

Squadrons of Cossacks, used by the Reds as they were by the Tsar, as mounted police, periodically surrounded villages in Pomerania and searched all the houses for deserters and stragglers who had remained behind with women. The Cossacks mercilessly drove the soldiers off to jail with their "nagaikas"—Cossack whips—but they kept the women for their own pleasure.[4]

In refusing Yamashita's plea for clemency General MacArthur in the following words condemned the Japanese leader for his maltreatment of the defenseless:

> The soldier, be he friend or foe, is charged with the protection of the weak and unarmed. It is the very essence and reason for his being. When he violates this sacred trust, he not only profanes his entire cult but threatens the very fabric of international society. The traditions of fighting men are long and honorable. They are based on the noblest of human traits—sacrifice.[5]

The Russians were not alone in violating these principles. Police records of Stuttgart show that during the French occupation, 1,198 women were raped and eight men violated by French troops, mostly Moroccans. Dr. Karl Hartenstein, prelate of the Evangelical church in the city estimated the number at 5,000. Frau Schumacher, secretary of the police woman's section, in submitting a documented report on numerous rapings, said that on the night the French evacuated the city a child of 9 was raped and killed, her mother also raped and shot, and her father killed by Moroccans. In the town of Vailhingen, with a population of 12,000, for example, 500 cases of rape were reported.[6] So it went in areas occupied by the French.

While a good number of American troops have resisted the example of others and deported themselves in a manner becoming their Christian backgrounds, the record for our occupation forces as a whole is dark.

An Associated Press dispatch from Nuremberg, Germany, quotes a letter which appeared in *Stars and Stripes* written by Capt. Frederick B. Eutsler, Chaplain of the 478th United States port battalion, charging that public behavior of American troops in Germany had become deplorable. He urged that the newspaper "launch a crusade against this disgraceful conduct which is earning a bad name for our army," and added, "I refer particularly to the assumption of many GI's that every German woman is immoral and it is their privilege to force their attentions on these women and insult them with indecent proposals.[7]

In April, 1946, the military authorities found it necessary to "crack down" and ordered stricter adherence to soldierly standards so as not to "discredit" the "fine performance of our troops in general."[8]

That same month an anonymous staff sergeant wrote in *Stars and Stripes* a charge that married men in the army were afraid to bring their wives to Germany because many American soldiers behaved like "supercharged wolves" toward women in public. He wrote: "Wise up, men. The hardest part of the war is now being fought, not with tommy guns, but with personalities. Let's show the Germans that we are men, not pigs."

In reporting the letter, Edward P. Morgan of the Chicago *Daily News* foreign service wrote:

> Whether he knew it or not the sergeant aired a subject which long has been a sore spot with American—and other—women in the European theatre. Ask almost any woman correspondent who has been around Europe at all and she will tell you reluctantly that the conduct of the average American soldier in public toward women is "disgraceful" compared to the reserve and discipline of his British, Russian, and French Allies.
>
> Now that spring has come to Bavaria, one of the favorite pastimes of the GI's in Nuremberg seems to be to drive slowly along the curb in jeeps and reach out and pat the posteriors of startled frauleins.[9]

When wives of men in our occupation forces arrived in Germany it became necessary, for their protection against indecent advances by American men, to wear special badges on their arms to distinguish them from German women.

One of the consequences of the immoralities of howling G.I. wolf packs is an upsurge in venereal diseases which has reached epidemic proportions. Before we arrived, although the rate had increased with the return of German soldiers from France and North Africa, it was still moderate and well under control—after our arrival, contamination soared. In December, 1945, only 7 per cent of German civilians receiving venereal disease treatment were men; by August, 1946, however, men constituted 41 per cent of the patients.[10] In other words, contamination had spread from our troops to the German women and finally to German men.

A large proportion of the contamination has originated with colored American troops which we have stationed in great numbers in Germany and among whom the rate of venereal infection is many times greater than among white troops. In July, 1946, the current rate of infections among white soldiers was 190 per 1,000 men per annum, meaning that slightly less than one in five would be infected in the course of a year. In contrast the rate among negro troops stationed in the American zone of Germany was 771 per thousand![11] In speaking of this general problem, Lee Hills, Chicago *Daily News* foreign correspondent, writes:

> Two of the biggest headaches in the American occupation of Germany are problems we brought with us. One is the extreme youth and inexperience our army men . . . The other problem—and one so politically touchy the War Department is afraid to remedy—is the heavy use of Negro American troops. The result, despite some superb Army leadership at the top, is that American prestige has steadily dropped from its V-E Day peak.
>
> The top men in Germany, almost without exception, think it's a mistake to have so many (42,000) Negro troops here. "They're simply not trained and disciplined for this job, which is vastly more complicated and delicate than fighting," said one general. "They have a higher crime rate, a venereal disease rate several times that of the white soldier, and a worse record for mischief in general . . . Frankly, the worst problem comes from our colored troops going with white German girls. This stirs bitter hatred among German men. Many of our own soldiers feel almost as strongly about it.[12]

That the German women do not accept advances from American troops out of choice but rather out of sternest necessity is shown by the close connection between the venereal disease rate and availability of food. As one correspondent writes:

> Statistics show that the venereal rate is related to the food supply of the German civilians during our occupation. After the winter's supply of potatoes was issued to the Germans last fall, there was a drop in the number of soldiers infected. As frauleins became more hungry, more soldiers were infected. Ration cuts last spring also were reflected in higher venereal figures.[13]

The German press broke its long silence on the subject of venereal contamination in a front page editorial in the *Neue Zeit*, a Soviet-licensed Berlin newspaper. The author, a young woman editor named Renate Lengnick, whose husband had not returned from the American zone of occupation, where he was a prisoner of war, struck at the collapse in moral foundations for sex relations: She wrote:

> There are husbands and sweethearts who have not yet returned. Many never will return. There are girls who will never have husbands. There is unemployment. Apprenticeships are empty promises. There is little to inspire hope.
>
> Thirty-five per cent of the civilian venereal disease victims are girls under 20. For most of them it was desperation that turned them to sex indulgence. They needed food, clothing, and shelter. Most important of what they lacked was hope for a normal, decent life.

> Doctors and police must continue their campaign of eradication without abatement. We must also rescue the spirit as well as the bodies of youth from demoralization.[14]

The main difference between American and Russian methods of ravishing the unconditionally surrendered women of Germany is the American capitalistic, free economy touch. The *Christian Century* for December 5, 1945, reports:

> The American provost marshal, Lieutenant Colonel Gerald F. Beane, said that rape represents no problem to the military police because "a bit of food, a bar of chocolate, or a bar of soap seems to make rape unnecessary." Think that over if you want to understand what the situation is in Germany.

Dr. George N. Schuster, President of Hunter College, charged, after a visit to the American zone:

> You have said it all when you say that Europe is now a place where woman has lost her perennial fight for decency because the indecent alone live.
>
> Except for those who can establish contacts with members of the armed forces, Germans can get nothing from soap to shoes.[15]

L.F. Filewood, writing in the *Weekly Review*, London, Oct. 5, 1945, stated:

> Young girls, unattached, wander about and freely offer themselves, for food or bed . . . Very simply they have one thing left to sell, and they sell it . . . As a way of dying it may be worse than starvation, but it will put off dying for months—or even years.[16]

Significantly, the *Potsdam Declaration* declares:

> The Allied armies are in occupation of the whole of Germany and the German people have begun to atone for the terrible crimes committed under the leadership of those whom in the hour of their success, they openly approved and blindly obeyed.

It fails to declare that the crimes to be committed by the Allied armies of occupation would eclipse those of which the Nazi armies have been accused. Now that the war is over and the heat of combat has died down enough to enable us to view the cold facts again, it must be brought home to the American people that much of what they have been led to believe was born of propaganda, that the German army, for example, actually behaved itself very correctly toward the people of occupied territories whose governments were signatories of the Hague and Geneva Conventions. The facts are now well known, and are beyond dispute, despite the opposite picture previously painted in the press as part of the horrendous business of war.

William L. Shirer, in his *Berlin Diary* (p. 412), on June 17, 1940, in the first flush of German occupation, described how many French women had fled Paris for fear of what the German armies might do to them.

> It seems, he wrote, the Parisians actually believe the Germans would rape the women and do worse to the men . . . The ones who stayed are all the more amazed at the very correct behavior of the troops—so far.

And their behavior never changed.

Frederick C. Crawford, President of Thompson Products, after a tour of inspection in which he, with others of the War Department, visited areas where the Germans had been in occupation for four years, in his "Report From the War Front, said:

> The Germans tried to be careful in their dealings with the people . . . We were told that if a citizen attended strictly to business and took no political or underground action against the occupying army, he was treated with correctness.[17]

CHAPTER SIX

The People Hunger

In view of all that has happened in Germany, it is small wonder that the people have been overtaken by extreme shortages of basic necessities, especially food.

Months after the war had ended and the conquerors had assumed complete control of the German government and therefore responsibility for the German people and their future, the Bishop of Chichester, quoting a noted German pastor, said:

> Thousands of bodies are hanging in the trees in the woods around Berlin and nobody bothers to cut them down. Thousands of corpses are carried into the sea by the Oder and Elbe Rivers – one doesn't notice it any longer. Thousands and thousands are starving in the highways . . . Children roam the highways alone, their parents shot, dead, lost.[1]

A wireless to the *New York Times* in April, 1946, says:

> Like Russia's half-wild vagabonds after World War I, Germany's youth is on the road . . . because there was not enough to eat at home. Homeless, without papers or ration cards . . . these groups rob Germans and displaced persons. They are . . . wandering aimlessly, disillusioned, dissolute, diseased, and without guidance.[2]

Despite conditions, the German people are putting up a brave struggle for existence. After a five-week tour of Europe, including Germany, Malcolm Muir, publisher of *Business Week*, told the Union League Club of Chicago:

> The Germans are making every effort to help themselves . . . It is not unusual to see a milch cow hitched to a plow, a woman leading the cow and a small boy guiding the plow.[3]

What harvesting machinery remains is mostly small, old fashioned and run down, often useless for want of parts. Draught work is supplied by animals and men. Oxen are used where available, and a horse and cow hitched together are common. It is not unusual to see a wagon of straw moving along a road with one or two old men at the tongue and a flock of women and children pushing. One observer writes:

> The plight of the Germans is epitomized by scenes in the stubble fields, which are thoroughly gleaned by the owners. Villagers, old men, women and children, may be seen picking up one grain at a time from the ground to be carried home in a sack the size of a housewife's shopping bag.[4]

Crop yields have been reduced by the five year fertilizer famine, which continues and the fact, as mentioned before, that the soil for the most part has been worked for 1,000 to 2,000 years.

Food reserves which were ample when the war ended were soon depleted, thanks in part to deliberate destruction by invading armies, and, in the case of the Russians and French, to armies of occupation living off the land. When we first invaded Normandy we were surprised by the large stores of food we found. It was the same elsewhere. Although his statement contrasted sharply with the current propaganda which had all Europe starving, Prof. Theodore Shultz of the University of Chicago, in November, 1943, had said that continental Europe that year had harvested good crops, that "farm production had been so well maintained despite the war that Europe will meet 90 to 95 per cent of her food requirements in the year after peace is declared."[5] Although distribution was disrupted at the end of the war, aggregate food stocks were large. But under Allied management they were soon dissipated.

The situation, worsened by the loss of the eastern "bread basket" and the large number of displaced persons and evacuees from the east, became critical and then catastrophic.

For six months our military government refused to supply any food from the outside to supplement the vanishing German stocks; however, the terrible consequences of this policy ultimately got under the tough hides of the occupation authorities to such an extent that by December they appealed to the U.S. Government to send sufficient food to prevent universal starvation. Relief was finally promised, and after many heartbreaking delays, a dribble arrived.

The intensity of the famine through which Germany is passing can be guaged by comparing the German diet with our own and with what experiments prove to be the minimum to maintain life.

An average slice of bread yields around 200 calories. The average American diet is 3,000 calories per person per day. To maintain weight and health, a lumberjack needs as much as 7,600 calories, an active woman at least 3,000.[6] Herbert Hoover, famed for his work in famine relief, says that 2,200 calories "is a minimum in a nation for healthy human beings."[7]

Various studies have been made to determine the effects of subnormal diets and the limits of starvation. The University of Minnesota conducted a test during the war in which a group of conscientious objectors voluntarily lived for several months on a daily diet of 1,650 calories. Within six months each man lost a fourth of his weight and experienced fainting spells, dizziness, and a feeling of always being cold. Their hearts shrank and some had to have two blankets even in summer. All lost three-fourths of their energy and work ability. "Each individual gradually tended to withdraw to himself, to shun social companionship . . . The main interest in life became the next meal."[8]

Northwestern University Medical School conducted a similar experiment with similar effects. A diet with protein and vitamin contents 40 per cent and 25 per cent of normal, respectively, was tried with results which in the words of Dr. Andrew C. Ivy, "hold out a dismal prospect for the people of food-restricted countries." He said little change was noted in the patients during the first month and a half; "after six weeks, however, they showed a slow, progressive deterioration in physical and mental health, accompanied by loss of endurance, skin lesions, leg pains, and mental slowness." It was difficult to get the subjects back to normal: "the time of recovery was in no case less than a month."[9]

In response to a question on the subject of minimum diets, the National Research Council States:

> The best evidence available to the Board would indicate that adult European males reduced to an intake on the average of 1,400 to 1,700 calories for a period of six months will suffer: 1) Reduction of capacity for work (endurance) to the point where only very light work can be performed effectively, moderate heavy work, and heavy work not at all. 2) Loss of power of mental concentration associated with apathy, depression, and a high level of irritability. 3) Increased susceptibility to infections and contagious diseases . . . The ability of a population to maintain or increase its own community production of food, not to speak of other goods, would be diminished. In the second place, there would be less hope of establishing acceptable community political organization. In the third place, a population subjected to such a low level of food supply might be expected to develop epidemics which might spread to other nations and consequently represent a hazard to the entire world.[10]

These facts prove the excruciating character of the rations imposed upon the German populace by the conquerors. In the American zone where the level has been consistently higher than in other zones the base ration since V-E Day has ranged between a high of 1,550 to a low of 1,180 calories per person per diem. Here is the record: before November 11, 1945, 1,262 calories; from that date through the following March, 1,550 calories; from April 1, 1946, through most of the following May, 1,275 calories; from then on through most of the summer, 1,180 calories. In August, 1946, it was raised to 1,350 calories, and in the fall was restored to 1,550 calories where it was supposed to remain during the winter of 1946-47.

Herbert Hoover in April, 1946, in commenting on the European situation in general called the 1,550 calorie level a "grim and dangerous base" and said: "At this level we believe most of the adults can come through the short period of four months until the next harvest. The children's health will become suceptible to disease. Many of the children and aged will fall by the wayside."[11] The consequences of keeping the base German rations at or below the 1,500 calorie level since V-E Day are not difficult to imagine. Although some of the German workers, such as farmers and miners, are allowed somewhat higher rations, the base ration applies to the great majority, including housewives and children. Such reports as the following made by an official of the food branch of the American Military Government should therefore cause no surprise.[12]

The greatest famine catastrophe of recent centuries is upon us in central Europe. Our Government is letting down our military government in the food deliveries it promised, although what Generals Clay, Draper, and Hester asked for and were promised was the barest minimum for survival of the people. We will be forced to reduce the rations from 1,550 calories to 1,000 or less calories.

The few buds of democracy will be burned out in the agony of death of the aged, the women, and the children.

The British and we are going on record as the ones who let the Germans starve. The Russians will release at the height of the famine substantial food stores they have locked up (300,000 to 400,000 tons of sugar, large quantities of potatoes).

Aside from the inhumanity involved, it is so criminally stupid to give such a performance of incredible fumbling before the eyes of the world. It makes all the many hard-working officers of the Office of Military Government, Food and Agricultural Branch, ashamed.

Karl Brandt.

Berlin, Germany, March 18, 1946.

The following is taken from a report prepared by the German Central Administration for Health, a German agency created by the Russian occupation authorities:

The people hunger. They hold only the immediate present responsible for their condition. They are without the energy to trace the links of causes. They have even forgotten Hitler. Beyond the immediate present their power to reproduce even memory does not reach. There is growing as though by psychological compulsion, a mass hysteria, with a thousand different symptoms of drug addiction, drunkenness, perversities, sadism, murder and infantilism . . . The situation is reaching a generally psycho-pathological state, through chronic hunger. We are seeing aberrations such as were previously known only among stranded and starving sailors in lifeboats, or thirsting persons forgotten by caravans in desert sands. It is increasingly impossible to discover in the masses of the people opinions. They have only animal urges.

The explanation of this mass phenomenon, this mental and spiritual paralysis, is physical. They are emaciated to the bone. Their clothes hang loose on their bodies, the lower extremities are like the bones of a skeleton, their hands shake as though with palsy, the muscles of the arms are withered, the skin lies in folds, and is without elasticity, the joints spring out as though broken.

The weight of the women of average height and build has fallen way below 110 pounds. Often women of child-bearing age weigh no more than 65 pounds. The number of still-born children is approaching the number of those born alive, and an increasing proportion of these die in a few days. Even if they come into the world of normal weight, they start immediately to lose weight and die shortly. Very often the mothers cannot stand the loss of blood in childbirth and perish. Infant mortality has reached the horrifying height of 90 per cent.[13]

The following dispatch from Wiesbaden, Germany, portrays the lot which has befallen the children:

> Those fat, round cheeked, chubby-legged German children so well known in picture and story—remember them?
>
> They're of another era. You do not see them now.
>
> I sat with a mother, watching her eight-year-old daughter playing with a doll and carriage, her only playthings. Then she came to supper—hard brown bread, three slim slices of pressed sausage, a cup of coffee substitute. Her legs were tiny, the joints protruding. Her arms had no flesh. Her skin drawn taut across the bones, the eyes dark, deep-set and tired.
>
> "She doesn't look well," I said.
>
> "Six years of war," the mother replied, in that quiet toneless manner so common here now. "She hasn't had a chance. None of the children have. Her teeth are not good. She catches illness so easily.
>
> "She laughs and plays—yes; but soon she is tired. She never has known"—and the mother's eyes filled with tears—"what it is not to be hungry."
>
> "Was it this bad during the war?" I asked.
>
> "Not this bad," she replied, "but not good at all. And now I am told the bread ration is to be less. What are we to do; all of us?
>
> "For six years we suffered. We love our country. My husband was killed—his second war. My oldest son is a prisoner somewhere in France. My other boy lost a leg. That's what the Nazis did for us. And now . . ."
>
> By this time she was weeping. I gave this little girl a Hershey bar and she wept—pure joy—as she held it. By this time I wasn't feeling too chipper myself . . . But it gives you an idea.[14]

Dr. Lawrence Meyer, Executive Secretary of the Lutheran Church, Missouri Synod, after returning from Germany said on January 13, 1946:

> Germany literally swarms with children. Eight children per family is nothing extraordinary. Millions of these children must die before there is enough food. In Frankfurt at a children's hospital there have been set aside 25 out of 100 children. These will be fed and

kept alive. It is better to feed 25 enough to keep them alive and let 75 starve then to feed the 100 for a short while and let them all starve.[15]

Dorothy Thompson reported:

In Berlin, in August, 1945, out of 2,866 children born, 1,148 died, and it was summer, and the food more plentiful than now . . . From Vienna a reliable source reports that . . . infant mortality is approaching 100 per cent.[16]

Edd Johnson of *P.M.*, on October 3, 1945, wrote from Germany:

The infant mortality rate if 16 times as high today as in 1943 . . . There is going to be a definite age group elimination. Most children under 10 and people over 60 cannot survive the coming winter.[17]

A United States Press dispach from Berlin, February 8, 1946, reads:

Official announcement that two German women had been murdered and their flesh sold on a food black market aroused fear today that organized gangs of human butchers were at work here. Spokesmen for the criminal investigation department of the German police said only two cases of murder-for-flesh had been established but that it was possible that butchers were operating on a much larger scale, killing their victims and peddling their flesh in local black markets.[18]

Hal Foust wrote from Berlin, February 20, 1946: "Germans are dying in masses, not so much from starvation alone as from illnesses aggravated by acute malnutrition."[19]

A United Press dispatch from Hamburg, Germany, March 22, 1946, reads:

33 workmen collapsed from hunger today—the first signs of starvation were apparent in this area—with hostility rising among the Hamburg working classes, and food riots continued in Hamburg for the fourth straight day.[20]

Dorothy Thompson wrote:

The children of Europe are starving. Six years of war, indescribable destruction, and the lunatic policies which have added to the disintegration inherited from the collapse of the Nazi regime have done their work. Germany, and with it Europe, is skidding into the abyss.

The facts are at last being revealed through what has amounted to a conspiracy of silence here . . . This war was fought by the

West in the name of Christian civilization, the Four Freedoms, and the dignity of man against those who were perpetrating crimes against humanity. But policies which must inevitably result in the postwar extermination of tens of thousands of children are also "crimes against humanity."[21]

General of the Army Dwight D. Eisenhower in November, 1945, solemnly warned that if our military victory is to have lasting significance, the United States and other nations must "assist the war devastated countries back on their feet." and added:

> If this bitter situation is not to become so disastrous as to make me wonder if it was worthwhile to have taken up arms against the Nazis, we in the United States—which is truly the land of plenty as compared to Europe—must be prepared to discharge a heavy responsibility.[22]

After giving Herbert Hoover, serving as Chairman of President Truman's Famine Investigating Commission, a grim report of Germany's food situation on April 13, 1946, Generals Joseph T. McNarney and Lucius Clay said in a formal statement:

> Political stabilty cannot develop under conditions which create political apathy. Political apathy can be overcome in a population which must devote its full effort to the daily search for food. Political stabilty in Germany is closely related to political stability in the rest of Europe.
>
> German transport facilities are required to move relief supplies and exports across Europe. German workmen must be used to man available transport facilities. German coal is vital to Europe. German potash, salt, lumber, spare parts, and other products are needed throughout Europe.
>
> Coal production in the Ruhr has declined substantially since the recent food cut. Without food Germany cannot produce coal. Without coal Germany cannot produce fertilizer and unless is produces fertilizer it cannot improve its food supply.[23]

The statement went on to point out that the American zone even in normal times had been a deficit area with regard to food, requiring 2,000,000 tons of imports in 1943-44. It said that the German economic pump must be primed with food imports, because the American zone and other western areas cannot produce enough to sustain life even at starvation levels.

Ten months after V-E Day, only 600,000 tons of food had been imported into our zone by AMG, or about one ounce per person per meal. Yet AMG officers asked GI's to remind the Germans that per meal. Yet AMG officers asked GIs to remind the Germans they owe America a debt of gratitude for feeding them.[24]

Evidence that the German Famine is Deliberate

Senator Homer E. Capehart of Indiana in an address before the United States Senate February 5, 1946, said in part:

> The fact can no longer be suppressed, namely, the fact that it has been and continues to be, the deliberate policy of a confidential and conspirational clique within the policy-making circles of this government to draw and quarter a nation now reduced to abject misery.
>
> In this process this clique, like a pack of hyenas struggling over the bloody entrails of a corpse, and inspired by a sadistic and fanatical hatred, are determined to destroy the German nation and the German people, no matter what the consequences.
>
> At Potsdam the representatives of the United States, the United Kingdom, and the Union of Soviet Socialist Republics solemnly signed the following declaration of principles and purposes:
>
> "It is not the intention of the Allies to destroy or enslave the German people."
>
> Mr. President, the cynical and savage repudiation of these solemn declarations which has resulted in a major catastrophe, cannot be explained in terms of ignorance or incompetence. This repudiation, not only of the Potsdam Declaration, but also of every law of God and men, has been deliberately engineered with such a malevolent cunning, and with such diabolical skill, that the American people themselves have been caught in an international death trap.
>
> For nine months now this administration has been carrying on a deliberate policy of mass starvation without any distinction between the innocent and the helpless and the guilty alike.
>
> The first issue has been and continues to be purely humanitarian. This vicious clique within this administration that has been responsible for the policies and practices which have made a madhouse of central Europe has not only betrayed our American principles, but they have betrayed the GIs who have suffered and died, and they continue to betray the American GIs who have to continue their dirty work for them.
>
> The second issue that is involved is the effect this tragedy in Germany has already had on the other European countries. Those who have been responsible for this deliberate destruction of the German state and this criminal mass starvation of the German people have been so zealous in their hatred that all other interests and concerns have been subordinated to this one obsession of

revenge. In order to accomplish this it mattered not if the liberated countries in Europe suffered and starved. To this point this clique of conspirators have addressed themselves: "Germany is to be destroyed. What happens to other countries of Europe in the process is of secondary importance."

These remarks were interspersed with a mass of supporting evidence.

There can be no question that there has been a deliberate attempt to keep the facts from the American public. Senator Eastland of Mississippi, for example, in a stirring address to the United States Senate December 3, 1945, exposing the chaotic conditions in Germany, told of the great difficulty he had encountered in gaining access to the official report on conditions in the Reich made by Calvin Hoover. He said the State Department at first refused to furnish him a copy of the report, but that through the intercession of a high official in the department he had been able to obtain it, but only "with the understanding and the promise received from me first that the information therein would be made available to the people of this country." Senator Eastland continued:

> There appears to be a conspiracy of silence to conceal from our people the true picture of conditions in Europe, to secrete from us the fact regarding conditions of the continent and information as to our policies toward the German people . . . Are the real facts withheld because our policies are so cruel that the American people would not endorse them?
>
> What have we to hide, Mr. President? Why should these facts be withheld from the people of the United States? There cannot possibly be any valid reason for secrecy. Are we following a policy of vindictive hatred, a policy which would not be endorsed by the American people as a whole if they knew true conditions?
>
> Mr. President, I should be less than honest if I did not state frankly that the picture is so much worse, so much more confused, than the American people suspect, that I do not know of any source that is capable of producing the complete factual account of the true situation into which our policies have taken the American people. The truth is that the nations of central, southern, and eastern Europe are adrift on a flood of anarchy and chaos.[25]

Victor Gollancz, influential left-wing British publisher and pamphleteer, in his book *Leaving Them to Their Fate—the Ethics of Starvation*, after marshalling voluminous proof explains the starvation in these words:

> The plain fact is when Spring is in the English air we are starving the German people, and we are starving them not deliberately in the sense we prefer their death to our own inconvenience.
>
> Others, including ourselves, are to keep or be given comforts while the Germans lack the bare necessities of existence. If it is a choice between discomfort for another and suffering for the German, the German must suffer; if between suffering for another and death for the German, the German must die.

He describes the ample British diet and stocks of food while the Germans starve and says:

> Stocks of food and feeding stuffs in this country owned and controlled by the minister of food, exclusive of stocks on farms or held by secondary wholesalers and manufacturers, were estimated to total on the last day of March no less than 4,000,000 tons.

He rejects the thesis that we should starve the Germans because they would have starved us had they won, on the ground that those who reason as the Nazis are no better than the Nazis. He could have added that starvation of children of an enemy country is to admit having enemy children. One leading daily thinks Mr. Gollancz fails to plumb the depths of the infamy:

> On the contrary it [the starvation] is the product of foresight. It was deliberately planned at Yalta by Roosevelt, Stalin, and Churchill, and the program in all its brutality was later confirmed by Truman, Attlee, and Stalin . . . The intent to starve the German people to death is being carried out with a remorselessness unknown in the western world since the Mongol conquest.[26]

Ample food stocks nearer to Germany even than those in England existed while the Germans starved. On the same page of a newspaper in the autumn of 1945 two articles appeared under the following headlines:

WEST GERMANS FACE HARD FIGHT AGAINST FAMINE

COME AND GET IT,
DENMARK TELLS HUNGRY EUROPE

The article under the latter reads:

> The exhausted Danish farming industry succeeded in increasing pigs to nearly two million, 60 per cent of the prewar stock, and last week 45,000 live cattle were offered to slaughtering, of which 32,000 had to be refused as the warehouses are filled to capacity and no shipping was available.

Denmark has, in vain, drawn the attention of Britain, the United States, and UNRRA to the facts, at the same time forwarding proposals, but no reply has been received so far.

The huge cold storage facilities in north Germany are not being utilized, and refrigerator ships are lying idle in north German harbors. At the same time slaughtering houses are forced to return live cattle to farmers, the cattle now consuming fodder that otherwise would be available to further increase production, as a result of the failure of distribution machinery.

Denmark would welcome it if public opinion would induce the united shipping pool, UNRRA and other concerned agencies to overcome difficulties and supply shipping essential to emptying "Europe's bursting larder."[27]

An Associated Press dispatch from Copenhagen a month earlier had told the same story:

While the rest of Europe hungers for meat, Denmark has 3,000 to 4,000 tons of surplus beef weekly which cannot be exported for lack of shippng space. Hoegsbro Holm, permanent secretary of the agricultural council of Denmark, said today that for the last six weeks farmers have had as many as 16,000 head of cattle ready for slaughter, but Denmark has been able to use and export only 10,000. Holm said, "We have been trying to get transport for at least two months but to date nothing is ready to take the meat."[28]

Another report, by Robert Conway of the *New York News*, written March 22, 1946, from Rome, under the headline: "Finds European 'Shortages' Are Exaggeration" reads:

Coincident with the arrival of former President Hoover on his food mission, it is timely and vital that the American public should receive the simple facts regarding the grossly exaggerated talk of shortages in Europe.

England is not starving, although food is short. France is better off than England, and Italy is better off than France. The rich and the racketeers are eating sumptuously in London, Paris, and Rome, and the poor in Italy have rations equivalent to the diet enjoyed in 1937 at the peak of Mussolini's prosperity era.

England is the only one of the three countries which is making an honest, serious effort to ration food and clothing and control prices. France is doing better than Italy, but the black market in Paris is flourishing in all lines of goods. Italy is exploiting everything in a fantastic black market based on the contempt of the majority of the nation for the ignorance of Allied—chiefly American—officers of language, customs, and the traditional system of bartering and begging.

> In addition, some officers are flagrantly cooperating in the various rackets.
>
> I found it possible to eat well and cheaply in London, Canterbury, and other English towns. I found a similar situation in Paris and its environs. Then I came to Italy which is a veritable land of plenty, although in all three countries black market restaurants supplied steaks, eggs, fruits and other delicacies at prices equivalent to those of restaurants in New York.
>
> The task of ferreting out the truth of the food and economic situation is a difficult one, and unless a better and more experienced personnel is supplied for the purpose than is evident in the permanent allied administration here, a distorted and inadequate picture will be given to Mr. Hoover.[29]

That the general European famine advertised by Washington is for the most part German, as reported by Senator Butler of Nebraska after a trip through 33 countries, is indicated by the fact that UNRRA has been used "to finance governments and not to feed the hungry." UNRRA has in effect supported these governments, mostly satellites of the Soviet Union, by supplying them with billions of dollars worth of goods which they, in turn, have *sold* to those with the money to buy, thus bringing to themselves handsome revenues in lieu of taxes.[30] In Germany, where there is widespread hunger and poverty, UNRRA is specifically forbidden to function for the benefit of any but "displaced persons," and then only by making requisitions against the starving Germans.[31] In August, 1946, Cyril Osborn, M.P., denounced the so-called relief agency of the United Nations as "the biggest racket in Europe."

For another thing, no Central Red Cross has been permitted to function in the stricken Reich. And it is now a matter of history that the Washington administration for nearly a year hotly resisted all efforts to bring private relief to the Germans, and only permitted a miserable dribble when it finally did allow it, at the urgent request of AMG officials. It placed the limit at 2,000 tons a month, limiting packages to 11 pounds and 72 inches in girth, with shipping charges of 14 cents a pound.

Senator Albert W. Hawkes, of New Jersey had made a strong appeal to the President urging that private relief packages be permitted to prevent mass starvation of the German people. In his reply, dated December 21, 1945, President Truman professed that "there is as yet no possibility of making deliveries of individual packages in Germany," because "the postal system and the communications and transportation systems of Germany are in the state of total collapse." He then said:

> Our efforts have been directed particularly toward taking care of those who fought with us rather than against us–Norwegians, Belgians, the Dutch, the Greeks, the Poles, the French. Eventually the enemy countries will be given some attention.
>
> While we have no desire to be ***unduly cruel to Germany***, I cannot feel any great sympathy for those who caused the death of so many human beings by starvation, disease, and outright murder, in addition to all the destruction and death of war. Perhaps eventually a decent government can be established in Germany so that Germany can again take its place in the family of nations. I think that in the meantime no one should be called upon to pay for Germany's misfortune except Germany itself.
>
> Until the misfortunes of those whom Germany oppressed and tortured are oblivated (*sic*), it does not seem right to divert our efforts to Germany itself. I admit that ***there are, of course, many innocent people in Germany*** who had little to do with the Nazi terror. However, the administrative burden of trying to locate these people and treat them differently for the rest is one which is almost insuperable. (emphasis added)[32]

This letter makes perfectly clear that we are deliberately discriminating against "the Germans," that Mr. Truman expected to be at least a little cruel in his treatment of them, and that he had not the slightest consciousness of the German children, as such, and the agonies they must suffer, although they surely "had little to do with Nazi terror" and certainly could be as easily located as Nazis and war criminals. It is difficult, indeed, to see how those responsible for our policy can escape condemnation under the following principles laid down by General Eisenhower:

> While I and my subordinates believe that stern justice should be meted out to war criminals by proper legal procedure, we would never condone inhuman or un-American practices upon the helpless, which is one of the crimes for which those war criminals must now stand trial.[33]

Michael Foote, M.P., in discussing this question reminded the House of Commons that there is an older law than any promulgated at Potsdam for the protection of victims or our policy:

> But who shall offend one of these little ones which believe in me, it were better for him that a millstone were hanged about his neck and that he were drowned in the depth of the sea.[34]

It later came out that Russian objection in the Control Council was at least partly responsible for our inability to send private relief packages to Germany. Four Senators, after being rebuffed at the White House in their request that the mails be opened to permit relief packages to Germany, learned that permission to do so must meet with unanimous consent of all four occupying powers and that the Soviet Union had opposed the idea. The four gave out this information in a statement which said in part:

> The American people should know once and for all that as a result of this government's official policy they are being made the unwilling accomplices in the crime of mass starvation. How long must we expect Mr. Stalin to deny your American people the opportunity to express their native humanitarianism and desires?[35]

Russia's inhuman truculence was referred to indirectly by General McNarney in a letter to Senator Wiley (February 14, 1946). He explained:

> United States citizens have not been permitted to send individual gift supplies to German nationals, as the establishment of international postal service, while under study, is yet to be effected.
>
> Once *such agreement* has been reached, the distribution of packages within the United States zone can be reasonably well met by the parcel post service which has now been reinstalled within Germany. (emphasis added)[36]

In other words, the difficulty was a question of *agreement*, rather than lack of facilities.

In close harmony with Russia's inhuman attitude, which had an ulterior purpose as part of a larger program, as we shall see, the "liberal" press has for the most part greeted with silence or derision all efforts to publicize the facts concerning German prostration and to bring relief to the suffering German masses. Eleanor Roosevelt, Senator Connelly, and the late Sidney Hillman, backed by personages in AMG, upon visiting Germany professed to see no evidence of starvation or suffering beyond what they considered tolerable. The New Republic expressed its horror over the possibility that Senator Wherry, who had agitated for a Senate investigation of conditions in Europe, including Germany, might become more influential. In the New Republic's own words, this was his crime: "His present efforts are devoted to getting more food for Germany and Austria."

In commenting on the New Republic attitude and PM's professed liberalism, William Henry Chamberlain, in his excellent article "The Crisis of Liberalism," which was entered in the Congressional Record, says:

> So it becomes a crime, in the eyes of a liberal magazine, to try to ward off what is at best acute malnutrition, at worse starvation. As to PM, with its loudly professed code of humanitarian ethics, it gives a daily exhibition, in its attitude toward relief for central Europe, of nazism in reverse, of a positively sadistic desire to inflict maximum suffering on all Germans, irrespective of their responsibility for Nazi crimes.[37]

"Liberals" have, however, indulged in some relief activities. Here is one case, as reported by correspondent Philip Warden:

> Washington, D.C., June 6 (1946)—The emergency food collection committee headed by Henry A. Wallace, Mrs. Eleanor Roosevelt, and Herbert Lehman, has collected $323,000 in cash and is incurring an estimated $300,000 in administrative expenses, Chairman Wallace reported to the Senate Small Business Committee today.
>
> Wallace listed among the "estimated cash requirements" for the two month campaign which is expected to wind up by July 1, $75,000 in salaries, $45,000 in travel and subsistence claims, $115,000 for publicity, materials, and stationery, $28,000 for communications, and $20,000 in state and metropolitan organizational expenses.[38]

CHAPTER SEVEN

Economic Tribulation

It is inconsistent to show solicitude for the welfare of Germany or the German people and at the same time to support the Potsdam agreements, because, as we have seen, the latter were intended not to help Germany recover but rather to prevent her from doing so. Potsdam was based on the Morgenthau Plan and the Morgenthau Plan had stipulated:

> The sole purpose of the military in control of the German economy shall be to facilitate military operations and military occupation. The Allied Military Government shall not assume responsibility for such economic problems as price controls, rationing, unemployment, production, reconstruction, distribution, consumption, housing, or transportation, *or take any measures designed to maintain or strengthen the German economy*, except those which are essential to military operations. The responsibility for sustaining the German economy and people rests with the German people with such facilities as may be available *under the circumstances*. (emphasis added)

"Under the circumstances" must be underscored as meaning an absence of essential facilities. The territorial losses and seizures; the program of over-crowding through expulsions of millions of eastern Germans; the wholesale enslavement of German manpower; the liquidation of German science and managerial, technical, and professional classes through de-nazification; the settling of the low level of industry decided upon, coupled with the industrial sacking and elimination of all German external resources—all these measures on top of the war devastation—

cannot be described as anything but a program to throw Germany and her people into a state of collapse.

But these are not the only acts of repression. Taxes have been raised to confiscatory levels which stifle incentives and prevent operation of the free enterprise system. They have helped to socialize German economy and kill the profit motive. They have corrupted public morals for even the poor must contrive to dodge them in order to have enough income to buy shoes.[1] We have refused to establish an exchange value for the German mark in terms of other currencies, preventing privately handled imports and exports and throwing what little external trade there is into the hands of the military government. And instead of trying to work out some intelligent plan for the resuscitation of the collapsed financial system we have proceeded to make matters far worse by such actions as the printing of vast sums of occupation currency which will almost certainly help create the 1923 inflation disaster and complete the destruction of the German middle class.[2] Such a result would serve the ends of Soviet Russia, but hardly those of the other powers.

Economic Prostration

It is difficult to imagine the depth of German depression. When the United States reached the bottom of 1932, industrial production had fallen to 60 per cent of normal. The depression was so severe—the losses so enormous, the unemployment so widespread—that it almost brought a revolution.

Industrial production in Germany a year after V-E Day was 10 per cent of what used to be normal.

Production in our zone has gradually risen until it reached a high of about 12 per cent of the old normal, or about 20 per cent of the new permitted levels. With the cut in rations, however, the index began a steady decline.[3] On May 4, Brig. Gen. William H. Draper, AMG director of economics, reported that output in our zone was "far below that necessary to maintain the minimum standard of living." The report went on to give production figures for individual industries as percentages of capacity. Here are a few samples: chemicals 25 per cent; electric power 20 per cent; building materials 20 per cent; steel products 13 per cent; ceramics 5 per cent; farm machinery 22 per cent; electrical equipment 15 per cent; automotive and industrial machinery 10 per cent.[4] The following summer it was reported that less than 30 per cent of available industry in our zone was in operation.[4]

Deputy Military Governor Clay at the end of August declared that it will take at least four more years for Germany to recover sufficiently to bring production up to the bare subsistence levels set under the deindustrialization program.[6]

War destruction plus the Allied program of repression have created thorough disorganization. Of the plants not bombed out completely, many were obsolete, others located in areas where residential destruction was so complete that there was no room for workers, or where available transportation and communications could serve only a fraction of production.[7] Freight carrying has been slow and unreliable, able to meet only 70 per cent of the low demand. Passenger service is covering only 30 per cent of German requirements. Cars are jammed and passengers even hang on the sides and tops. Railroad shortages lie in rolling stock, ships, manpower, coal, and result in part from bottlenecks and the inevitable inefficiency of military control.[8]

Low coal production has been a key problem resulting in part from lack of civilian goods available to miners and their families. The AMG official in charge said in July, 1946, that the miners must be fed better and treated better in other ways to get improved output.

> We are going to have to provide decent housing and we are going to have to make consumer goods available, as an incentive for the miners to dig. At present they cannot even buy needle and thread with which to patch their pants . . . There is no slowdown conspiracy nor underground political sabotage by the workers, it is just that they have not enough incentive to work.[9]

A high ranking British officer a few days earlier had admitted that anti-British sentiment is growing in the Ruhr. He said:

> The Germans are just beginning to appreciate the economic hardships imposed upon them by allied policy. It is natural there should be a stiffening of the German attitude toward this policy, and that the British should receive the brunt of this stiffening since the reparation program takes more from the British zone than from other parts of Germany.

He pointed out that the miners lack incentive due to the absence of food and other necessities and added: "In a vicious economic cycle we do not have consumer goods because manufacturing plants lack the coal to make them. Therefore we must have more coal for production.[10]

Bottlenecks and shortages permeate the whole German economy as the inevitable consequence of war destruction and the production prohibitions enforced under the level of industry plan. In July, 1946, for example, it was reported that the metal shortage had halted the production of plows, while the supply of horseshoes and nails was about exhausted. The number of motor trucks in Berlin, with its 3,000,000 inhabitants and area five times that of Chicago, was down to 8,000. Solder was not available even for mending pots and pans. Shoe cobblers were using old portfolios, dice boxes, helmet liners, any piece of salvage leather they could find to repair shoes. Although 50,000 school children were out of shoes, the supply of shoe nails was about exhausted. Because of lack of permanganate of potash, caused by dismantlement of I.G. Farben plants, the manufacture of saccharine, vitally needed on account of the sugar famine as well as by diabetics, was threatened. Manufacture of adhesive tape, muslin, bandages, and surgical dressings was halted in Thuringia because cotton mills appropriated by the Russians would not furnish raw materials. Cement production, sorely needed for reconstruction, was low because of dismantlements and shortage of machinery and tools.[11] Reports reveal that such industries as rug, fabric, cutlery, toy, and musical instrument factories, fortunate to have survived the war, lack fuel and raw materials.[12]

Current German production has been far less than enough to supply current minimum needs of the populace. For the first year, it was possible to draw on reserve supplies left over from pre-surrender days and spared in the looting and destruction even of vast leftover food stores by the armies of the victors.[13] But these reserves were gradually exhausted, leaving a dark prospect for the future. Clothes wore out and could not be replaced, due to the virtual nonexistence of textiles for civilian use. In consequence, as one report put it: "The best dressed frauleins in Berlin this spring will wear a combination of window curtains and old bedclothes."[14]

Desperation for money to buy food on the black markets to supplement the starvation rations, has led the Germans to sell their assets, disposing first of what they need the least. Their rings have gone, then watches, bracelets, that other pair of shoes, dresses, jackets, suits. As one Berlin reporter put it:

> Last winter there was no coal, and Berliners burned every tree in town and for several miles around. Cold is the most miserable of all living conditions, and as people get closer and closer to the primitive, it's natural that they look to the future. At first I was amazed to see girls walking down Berlin streets in summer clad in long coats of fox, or squirrel, or sheep. Then I realized. Remembering last winter; looking toward another winter without fuel—the've sold the clothing least needed. And I'm not kidding when I say a lot of these frauleins are down to their last fur coat.[15]

Associated Press bulletin from Hereford, Germany, dated September 9, 1946 reads: "The British officially informed Germans in their zone today they could expect no coal for heating this winter."[16]

A little later an arrangement was made for miners to work Sundays, so that the average family of four in the merged American and British zone could have fuel this winter equivalent in heating value of a little over half a ton of hard coal for a six months period.[17] A month later the unions voted not to work on Sundays.

In the face of this grim prospect, the best that could be hoped for in the way of food by the population living on the very edge of starvation, suffering from famine edema, swelling of joints, and all the other terrors of gradual starvation, as stated before, was an increase in rations to the "grim and dangerous" 1,500 calorie level throughout the 1946-47 winter. In June, 1946, Col. H.B. Hester, in charge of the American military government food branch, predicted a disastrous famine in Germany the next winter unless the ration level was raised by October.[18] His report followed another by Col. W.L. Wilson, chief of public health and welfare, that the condition of the conquered people was sinking rapidly under the present ration.[19]

In the French zone 5,000 have died weekly of starvation.[20] In mid-summer of 1946, in Berlin, 19,000 very serious tuberculosis cases for whom no beds were available were reported officially by American authorities. The Senate of Hamburg issued an appeal to England and the entire world to send food and medicines to "avert terrible epidemics and mass deaths." Hamburg motormen and conductors were imperiling safety of public transport by "fainting from hunger" and dropping at their posts from long undernourishment and weakness while on duty. The Medical Council of Cologne informed the British military authorities that the population there "is facing catastrophe" unless food was quickly provided, adding that "resistance to infectious diseases, especially tuberculosis, is vanishing." Authorities in the Rhineland sent an appeal from Düsseldorf to the Brtitsh military government to "close the murderous food gap," in order to check rapidly spreading disease and epidemics caused by hunger." A medical authority said:

> Many thousands of men, women, and children, who, with what reserves in strength and vitality they still possessed, managed to live through the rigors, cold and hunger of last winter, will not survive this winter, after another year's depletion in their power of resistance to diseases fostered by starvation and semi-starvation. Death's harvest indeed may be appalling.[21]

With this frightful prospect it will behoove relief organizations to operate at maximum capacity if millions of lives are to be saved.

Economic Dismemberment

Big Four officials have laid all the blame for Germany's distress on the war and zonal separation. In their view Potsdam would afford the best possible solution to all difficulties if only zonal division could be corrected.

German territory west of the Oder-Neisse line was divided into four zones to be occupied and administered by the military forces of Russia, Great Britain, the United States, and France:

Russia's zone, comprising the eastern half of Prussia west of the Oder-Neisse river line is the best balanced of the four zones. In addition to containing some 45 per cent of Germany's manufacturing during the war, it produced more than enough food for its own consumptiom and mines brown coal and other minerals. Other sections of the Reich had been heavily dependent upon it for many key raw materials and manufactures. Stripped as it has been, it nevertheless supplies Russia with a sizable flow of goods taken as reparation.

Britain's zone comprises the western half of Prussia. Within it is the Ruhr District which contains the continent's most valuable natural resources, especially large deposits of high grade coal close to Europe's best iron ores, and lies in the midst of Europe's densest concentration of population in a region served by excellent rail and water transportation. Molotov rightly called it "Europe's workshop." Despite intensive cultivation the zone suffers a heavy food deficit, and even coal production has been at a low ebb since V-E Day. Administration costs are 320 million dollars a year above revenues.

The American zone lies in the central and southern sections of the Reich. Most of it is mountainous and largely scenic. It is not and cannot become self-sufficient in food production and is highly dependent upon various imports. It perfectly illustrates the essential interdependence of all sections of German economy. All of its hard coal requirements must be imported from the Ruhr or Saar regions, and 83 per cent of the steel required by its many manufacturing establishments must come from the outside. Lack of coal has forced partial or total closing of many industries; for example, the pharmaceutical industry, which needs coal tar; the tire business, which needs buna made from coal; and various fabricating, processing and finishing establishments. Because of the steel shortage, the largest tin can manufacturer in Bavaria closed so that some 10 million tins badly needed to put up the 1946 crop of peas, beans, and fruit, were not made. Large numbers are unemployed and administration is costing the American taxpayers 200 million dollars a year.

France's zone consists mostly of provincial fragments of former Germany bordering on France and contains no complete political or economic entities.

Its chief asset is the Saar Basin, rich in coal and steel. Although intensively cultivated, the zone is not self-sufficient in food, because of heavy specialization in vineyards and orchards. It must import its potatoes from Bavaria, for example, and other zones rely upon its food specialties.

One of the outstanding facts about Germany is the dependence of each section, and now each zone, upon all the others—for food, steel, coal, timber, and other essentials. The peace settlements did not anticipate economic separation of Germany's highly interdependent regions. Since the zones were set up strictly for administrative purposes and were not supposed to exert any divisive influence upon Germany economy, zonal boundary lines were laid out promiscuously across political and economic subdivisions. The belief that the zones would remain one thing and

German economy another is clearly shown in the early statements and declarations of policy.

Potsdam directs that "during the period of occupation *Germany shall be treated as an economic unit,*" and an earlier Big Four statement on control machinery for Germany decrees that:

> The Control Council, whose decisions shall be unanimous, will ensure appropriate uniformity of action by the Commanders in Chief in their respective zones of occupation and *will reach agreed decisions on the chief questions affecting Germany as a whole.*

This demand for results made impossible by the conditions laid down simultaneously has been about as effective as commanding the sun to stand still.

Insisted upon by Russia the requirement that Control Council decisions "shall be unanimous" has in practice barred "agreed decisions on the chief questions affecting Germany as a whole," and has brought anything but uniformity of zonal action. It has killed Control Council effectiveness just as the veto power also insisted upon by Russia has destroyed the effectiveness of the Security Council of the United Nations Organization.

France has been particularly obstructive in Control Council voting. Although British and American delegations insisted upon inclusion of France in the Four Power control and occupation of the Reich, France has never signed the Potsdam agreements. In consequence she is not bound by the agreements, yet is able to veto their execution.[22] She has frankly admitted her opposition to German unification and, for her own presumed self-protection and territorial aggrandizement, has demanded that Germany be Balkanized and destroyed as a power factor of Europe. To achieve this end she had obdurately insisted, as mentioned before, that the whole of western Germany be broken off and either internationalized or added to France. Upon taking her place among the Big Four, she served notice that until these demands were met, she would veto all Control Council decisions aiming to treat the Reich as an economic unit and thereafter lived up to her promise—even to such a fine point as rejecting a national postage stamp.

France has been by no means alone in blocking unified economic administration. Russia has been almost as obstructive and would probably have been more so had France not been so obliging. Even

Britain and the United States have not hesitated to balk whenever it appeared selfishly advantageous for them to do so.

In the absence of "agreed decisions" calling for uniform action in all zones, the Reich has become divided into four economically deficient and unbalanced "air tight" compartments, each administered exclusively by its occupying power as though it were a colony or protectorate. More difficult to surmount than those of independent states, zonal boundaries form such barriers to interzonal intercourse that what little trade occurs must be barter deals arranged by special treaty.[23]

Although such economic dismemberment would alone guarantee economic disorganization, it cannot rightly be made to serve as a scapegoat for all the sins of Potsdam, nor for the British and American zonal deficits. Even in the absence of zonal separation the other harsh and repressive measures ordered at Potsdam would assure German economic paralysis.

Disregarding this manifest fact, many officials find it convenient to lay all the blame on the zonal barriers and to argue that if they could be eliminated Potsdam would be transformed from a dismal failure into a dazzling success. The thesis may enable them to avoid admitting the colossal blunder Potsdam really is, but it also serves as a bar to taking the steps necessary to meet the trouble fundamentally.

Put forward as a general panacea for all German administrative ills, economic *anschluss* of as many zones as possible has become the chief objective of our zonal authorities. In the attempt to break down French and Russian objections, they offered to divide the Reich into a number of federated states and to guarantee German disarmament for 25 or even 40 years. After this proposal was rejected on the ground that it was wholly inadequate and would lead to war, they offered to merge the American zone economically "with one, two, or three other zones."[24] In making the offer, AMG Commander-in-Chief, General McNarney observed:

> The United States Government proposed this arrangement because of its belief that Germany can no longer be administered in four air tight compartments without free economic intercourse, unless paralysis is to result. The United States Government is unwilling to permit creeping economic paralysis to grow if it is possible to attain economic unity between its zone and any other zone in Germany, as a prelude to economic unity for all Germany.[25]

Although Russia and France turned down the offer, Britain accepted and the task of effecting economic unification of the British and American zones was undertaken.

Even if such an economic merger can be made, effective in the absence of political unification, which is doubtful, it is but one short step in a long way that must be traveled before substantial permanent amelioration of Germany's plight can be attained. On the other hand, the merger partitions the Reich between East and West and intensifies and embitters the conflict between the two.

CHAPTER EIGHT

Teaching Democracy in Reverse

The Lord High Executioners

We thought we were coming to Germany as liberators to free the German people from dictatorship, to teach them the errors of their ways, and to give them the benefits of our form of democracy and free enterprise. Actually we accepted at Potsdam a program which negated all of our principles, which could sell our form of democracy only in reverse. The Potsdam plan was made to order for Soviet Russia, but not for free enterprise or free democratic processes. Its very execution requires totalitarianism of the kind the Soviets are accustomed to, of the kind which, when the Nazis were practicing it, so outraged us that we fought a half trillion dollar war to eradicate it from the earth.

We first eliminated the German government, the only instrumentality through which the German people might take collective self-preservative action and then substituted a system of military absolutism, born not of free American institutions or ideals, but of the absolutisms dominant at Potsdam. Military absolutism was set up under the following edict:

> In the period when Germany is carrying out the basic requirements of unconditional surrender, supreme authority in Germany will be exercised, on instruction from their Governments, by the Soviet, British, United States, and French Commanders-in-Chief, each in his own zone of occupation, and in matters affecting Germany as a whole. The four Commanders-in-Chief will together constitute the Control Council.

Set up to function under the heads of this alien military dictatorship is a complicated bureaucracy headed by a hierarchy of descending Caesars, forming a neat replica of the authoritarian apparatus employed by both the Soviets and Nazis.

This dictatorship, as we have seen, has as its purpose not the resuscitation and rehabilitation of the fallen Reich, but rather its repression and the erection of barriers to recovery. With hundreds of thousands of heavily armed occupation troops behind it, the alien dictatorship was also prepared to prevent resistance by the Germans as they saw the ground prepared for their extermination by their being thrown on their own, and forbidden outside assistance while the necessary means for their survival were destroyed. It has dropped a soundproof iron curtain down around its victims, virtually cutting off intercourse with the outside world, ostensibly to prevent contamination of other nations by Nazi ideas, but also to prevent the anguished cries of the German women and children from reaching and disturbing others while the gruesome program was carried into effect.

As the death noose tightened about them, the Germans were to be made to believe they are entirely to blame for their dilemma. Even the inevitable economic collapse must be laid at the door of German administrators. They must be made to spring their own trap door. Potsdam says:

> In the imposition and maintenance of economic controls . . ., German administrative machinery shall be created and the German authorities shall be required to the fullest extent practicable to proclaim and assume administration of such controls. Thus it should be brought home to the German people that the responsibility for the administration of such controls and *any breakdown in these controls will rest with themselves.* (emphasis added)

This was the craven way we were to bring self government to the Germans.

We no doubt hoped, for example, that by turning denazification over to so-called "German" prosecutors and courts set up and operating under our mandate we could make the Germans blame themselves for the deleterious effects.

We have said it is democratic to make the Germans conduct their own purge, which is tantamount to accepting the Russian purges as democratic. But those purges were at least Russian affairs. The German purge machinery is operated by Communists and radical

Marxist Socialists placed in office by an alien dictatorship and no more representative of the Germans than Quisling's Nazi government was of the Norwegians. The Germans know full well that whatever our puppets do reflects our will and dicta. If we should by any chance convince them that this is what we mean by the democracy we came to force upon them, we could hardly blame them if they rejected it at the first opportunity.

Our military government is anything but democratic, except in the Russian sense. It is headed by well-trained military men, competent to carry out military tasks and orders received from Washington prepared by politicians and behind-the-scenes operators. Instead of a democratic body representative of free Americans, they are order takers, willing to carry out without question whatever directive they receive from above. They are identical in this respect with Hitler's loyal hierarchy of lord high executioners.

Our troops of occupation have been splendid young American boys, but for the most part raw, inexperienced, teenage draftees who could be expected neither to relish their job nor to comprehend its exacting nature. The whole experience has tended to corrupt and brutalize them. As mentioned before, our use of a disproportionate number of negro troops has helped alienate the Germans and disgust our own personnel.

In conjunction with the military forces we have sent over a corps of high salaried civilian employees, consisting in large measure of people who had failed in the social and economic competition at home, including in some cases broken down, discharged officers who could not stand the rough going of actual combat in France and Italy, or the chagrin of having to return home as failures before the war was over, but who now draw higher pay than ever in their lives during peacetime before, and who enjoy swelling arrogantly with self-assumed importance before defeated but often more refined, cultured, and substantial people caught under their delegated authority.

This motley crew for the most part has no intimate knowledge of European and especially German conditions, mores, problems, or history, but was hastily recruited and superficially trained for its extremely demanding mission.

Although circumstances do not permit our body of civilian employees as a whole to be representative of the best there is in America, there are, fortunately, some notable exceptions. Often at great personal sacrifice, some very able, well-informed, conscientious experts and specialists have gone over and by their influence and efforts helped to mitigate the difficult situation. To these splendid products of our free institutions must go the lion's share of credit for whatever success AMG has achieved. For army men, if they are competent as such, cannot be expected to manage and perform major operations on a crippled foreign economy and social system without creating chaos. If the Army has proved unequal to the task of running such relatively simple things as railroads and mail order houses in America, it surely must be unequal to the stupendous job given it in Germany.

Potsdam has imposed upon us a program which runs counter to our fundamental convictions and philosophy. The military men who head AMG generally believe that the less government interferes with business the better it is for everybody, except in Germany. And they oppose collectivism philosophically, except in Germany. Although they fought a war to destroy dictatorship, they are willing to serve as one themselves and to impose almost complete control over the lives of individual Germans. Nothing runs without their permission.

Zonal rule over the economic, political, and cultural life of the German people, as commanded at Potsdam, could be handled with a modicum of success only by men with long experience in totalitarian philosophy and methodology. And in this respect the Russian zonal authorities enjoy a great advantage. Whereas the rule which Potsdam orders is alien to our background, training, and philosophy, it conforms perfectly to Russian practice at home. Such rule cannot bring free enterprise to Germany; only some form of collectivist society could grow up under it.

These are points of cardinal importance in the rivalry between Soviet Russia and the western powers over ultimate control of the German Reich.

"Reeducation"

Many ardent supporters of Potsdam have become greatly upset about Communist plans for taking over the Reich. They have no right to be, because the very first signature affixed to the document is that of Joseph Stalin. The Russians, therefore, have just as much right as we to lay down the meaning of its loose provisions and undefined terms. When Potsdam calls for democratization of the Reich without specifying exactly what is meant by "democracy," the Soviets have a perfect right to insist that the order calls for German communization. And this is but one of the pernicious features of its "re-education" program.

Potsdam, in connection with denazification, decrees that ousted Nazis "shall be replaced by persons who by their political and moral qualities, are deemed capable of assisting in developing genuine democratic institutions in Germany." But no hint is given as to what "genuine democratic institutions" might be. It prohibits propagation of national socialist ideas, without stating what they are, and then provides that "German education shall be so controlled as completely to eliminate Nazi and militarist doctrines and to make possible the successful development of democratic ideas," again without definition.

But forbidding propagation and discussion of one political philosophy and forcing the public to accept a different one held by those in the seats of power is Nazi doctrine. It is also Communist doctrine. And the Communists claim theirs is the one and only genuine democracy.

Political democracy, say the Bolsheviks, is impossible over the long run without "economic democracy," by which they mean abolition of private ownership of property, the foundation of free enterprise. But they call free enterprise fascism, and defenders of the American system fascists. And Nazism is a form of fascism. Denazification, in Russian eyes, therefore, is tantamount to rooting out our own system, along with all other private property systems.

The Bolsheviks call any country or party fascist or Nazi if it takes or advocates measures to curb the activities of Communist parties; those which permit the Communists to go freely about their business of destroying them and building a world soviet union are denominated "democratic." Thus, Potsdam qualifies as a "democratic" document.

These facts were known, or should have been known, by all the principals at Potsdam. When Russia was permitted to sign the agreements without a clear definition of what was meant by "democracy," we were falling into a dangerous trap from which we cannot escape, unless we simply repudiate the agreements we signed. The whole thing makes us look very stupid.

If by democracy we meant ***our*** way of life—free enterprise, private property, individual liberties, the protections guaranteed in the Bill of Rights, and government of, by, and for the people—it should have been obvious to us from the beginning that the program to establish democracy by force was foredoomed to failure. We might logically have hoped to wipe out Hitlerism by Hitlerite methods, but we certainly could never hope to establish our way of life that way.

Our intolerance of Nazi political opinion, however justified it may seem, is nevertheless the opposite of democratic in the American sense. Our determination to wipe out ideas by force is a repudiation of democracy's most sacred tenets. People who really believe in freedom of thought and opinion do not use clubs on the debating platform. We despised Hitler for burning books proscribed by the Nazis, not because we were necessarily partial toward the particular books involved, but as a matter of principle. Yet we have ourselves violated the principle, and adopted Hitler's, by burning the Nazi books. In words we denounce Hitlerism; in deeds we exonerate it!

The impression has been given by prolonged propaganda that national socialist tenets were obviously evil and criminal, that they openly called for aggressive war, for example, and conquest of the world. This is not true. Like the platform of any political party seeking support at the polls, its planks appeared to be quite innocuous. In fact, Nazism and its works were praised by many foreign notables such as Lloyd George and Winston Churchill. When polled, 51 per cent of our own GI's, stationed in Germany, said they believed Hitler "did the Reich a lot of good before 1939," and 19 per cent of those questioned believed "the Germans had some or a good deal of justification for starting the war." "It showed large percentages of the soldiers ready to accept German explanations and willing to absolve the mass of Germans from responsibility for concentration camp atrocities." "29 per cent conceded they had grown 'more favorable' toward their former enemies since they had been in the country."[1]

It was perfectly possible for honest, intelligent, conscientious German citizens to be party members and even enthusiasts. For us to assume differently is merely to exhibit our ignorance and gullibility for propaganda. Nazism was wrong in many fundamental respects, and these features should be exposed. The Germans should be shown in principle where these ideas were wrong and dangerous. They should be stated as general principles to be opposed no matter who advances them, even if they are communists. And the operation should be discussion, by free, uncensored debate. Certainly, nothing can be gained by treating the subject as undiscussable.

The Nazis were wrong in their invasion of the schools and forcing elimination of certain ideas and texts and acceptance of certain others. They were wrong in principle. So are we, when we impose our ideas and textbooks on the Germans. We are even more so for being outsiders, whereas the Nazis were at least German. The Nazis were wrong in their strict censorship of the German press. And so are we. We cannot create a free press in Germany through rigid censorship and we look very foolish when we try it.

Persecution of people on account of their blood is deplorable—whether practiced by the Germans or against them. Persecution arises from hate and is stirred by hatemongers. Walter Winchell has said we must hate the Germans. "Let future German generations see them [German monuments] and find out what kind of blood they were born with," he wrote a year after Germany surrendered. "If they can grow up among reminders of what it costs to be a monster, maybe they'll work a little harder to get back into the human race."[2] Likewise, while Secretary of State Byrnes was appealing to the Germans at Stuttgart, the information and education department of the U.S. Army in the European theatre was still calling for hatred toward the German people. In a pamphlet it said:

> The feeling of pity for the Germans is very similar to the psychological reaction we get toward a pretty girl who murdered her father in cold blood, owing to the reluctance to condemn one who looks so nice and kind, as a murderess.

The Germans in their hate mongering were no more unheedful of the Christian, "Love thine enemy."

The German leaders applied the hideous and indefensible doctrine of collective guilt against a whole people whom they looked upon as deadly enemies. This was one of their greatest crimes. We have committed the same crime by applying the same doctrine against all the people of Germany, including unborn babes. Perhaps the reason we forbid discussion of Nazism, fail to list its features, and try to destroy it by force, goes back to our having unconsciously accepted most of its worst features since 1932, without knowing their identity.[3]

And so we go blithely on our way trying to stamp out Nazism while practicing it ourselves. The very stamping is Nazi-like.

We came as liberators to teach the Germans how to enjoy self-government and political freedom. Yet we have imposed our denazification decrees which so frighten them that they refuse to take part in politics for fear of the possible consequences under our "democratic" control. We are trying to teach them democracy, and yet we have so circumscribed what they may teach that their teachers, unless they are Communists, are afraid to say anything. Politically, German leaders are not permitted to speak freely, and even those in our military government are afraid to say what they think, for fear of the consequences. Because of our undemocratic policies regarding freedom of the press, which we preach while violating in practice, the German press is operating in a vacuum. Intellectual hunger in Germany is almost as acute as physical hunger.

On top of everything else, our system of justice has become brutalized and highly discriminatory. We have three separate bodies of laws, one for our forces, one for displaced persons, and one for the German population, and in none is there a serious effort to make the punishment fit the crime. For example, a frail, widowed, German mother of two small children was sent to jail for five months for having in her possission a parachute knife given her as a trophy and remembrance by her husband just before he was shot down over Britain.[4] This is typical, not exceptional. It makes the Germans shudder at "democratic justice." While we preach law and order, we coddle and grant special privileges to "displaced persons," who according to AMG officers, have been responsible for 50 per cent of the crimes in the American zone.[5]

While preaching democracy we have installed ourselves as an alien plutocracy, many of whose members have found blackmarket operations and other shady deals not beneath them. While the Germans around them starve, wear rags, and live in hovels, the American aristocrats live in often unaccustomed ease and luxury. Their wives must be specially marked to protect them from licentious advances; they live in the finest homes from which they drove the Germans; they swagger about in fine liveries and gorge themselves on diets three times as great as they allow the Germans, and allow "displaced persons" diets twice as great. When we tell the Germans their low rations are necessary because food is so short, they naturally either think we are lying to them or regard us as inhuman for taking the lion's share of the short supplies while they and their children starve.

We have in many ways shown ourselves quite callous to the sufferings of the conquered. The war left in its wake countless numbers of war victims with disabled bodies, some without arms, legs, eyes, or otherwise disfigured. They and the millions killed in battle or held as war prisoners have millions of dependents, aged parents, wives and children. In addition there are the hordes of impoverished, suffering expellees from the east. But the towering needs of all these millions of helpless Germans have been a minor consideration to the feeding and housing of displaced persons. Only a little news comes from their loved ones held as war prisoners in England, France, and other western countries, none from Russia. Nor has the Allied Control Council yet issued a full and detailed list of either war casualties or war prisoners. Thousands are still held in unnecessary, agonizing suspense wondering whether fathers and brothers who were in the war are still alive or dead. As one German mother said," Even a little sympathy would help. I haven't heard from my son for more than a year now. If I knew he were dead, I could get over it."

This is the way to teach democracy in reverse. If the Germans are ever to become adherents, they must do so voluntarily, through conviction, not compulsion. By our behavior we are making it impossible for them to gain the conviction. In the light of what they are having to endure under our control and because of our policies and weaknesses, they will not easily conclude, as we wish them to, that Hitlerism is uniquely brutal, oppressive, or dishonest.

One of the main difficulties is the fact that our democracy is confronted by a paradox which almost defies solution. Far from facing or solving it, we have failed to notice it. And those whom we wish to win to democratic principles see our blindness and lose their respect for their would-be teachers. We must sooner or later make up our minds whether democracy can tolerate the spread of democracy-destroying doctrines, and if not, how it can stop them and still remain democracy.

If what we are doing in Germany against Nazism is right, then what we are doing here at home about Communism is wrong. If we must stamp out Nazism there, we must stamp out Communism here; if in the name of democracy and freedom of opinion we can tolerate dissemination of Communist doctrine and treasonable Communist fifth column activities here, we should treat Nazism with equal kindness over there. For the one is just as bad as the other.

CHAPTER NINE

The Kremlin's Program

Imperialist Expansion and World Revolution

To comprehend Russia's bid for control over the German Reich, it is necessary first to have an understanding of the Soviet Union's more general aims and ideas. Lack of such knowledge is primarily responsible for the botch our leaders have made of our relations with Moscow.

Surging, aggressive Soviet Russia represents a merger of the territorial ambitions of old Russian imperialism and the communist program of world revolution. The former proceeds as before on military power and the allurements of Pan-Slavism, to which has now been added the force of world communism. The latter, motivated as always by the crusading urge of ideological fanaticism, finds itself carried along by the expansionist imperialism of its base, Soviet Russia. Reinforcing each other as they do, the two confront the world with menacing power.

Russian imperial expansion, now as in former years, threatens British trade routes, strategic oil reserves, and commercial opportunities. Russian attempts to penetrate through Iran to the Persian Gulf and through the Dardanelles and Trieste to the Mediterranean are to Britain intolerable threats to her lifeline to India. Equally damaging is the actual and potential enlargement of the Soviet Union itself, for wherever it expands it virtually closes the door to international trade and financial operations on which Britain thrives and without which she starves. Through the force of world communism the U.S.S.R., which has already drawn into its orbit the eastern half of Europe and important sections of Asia, actively menaces other sectors all over the globe – in Asia, Africa, western Europe, and even the Americas.

And because we believe our own vital interests parallel those of Britain, our reaction to Russian expansion is similar to the British and collaborates closely with it.

World Communism, based on the teachings of Marx, Lenin, and now Stalin, paints capitalism as a diabolical exploitative system in which the propertied classes rob the workers through the wage system. In harmony with Marx's dialectical materialism and economic teachings, Communists and many Socialists believe that capitalism is dying by predestined, convulsive stages involving commercial crises, wars, and catastrophes, that the end of the capitalist world is at hand, to be superseded by a new world order of socialism.

Communists deem it their mission to hasten by all available means the process of capitalist disintegration and the advent of the socialist millennium. Following the philosophy that might makes right, that the end justifies the means, their every act, even when disguised as "reform," is calculated to hasten the revolutionary downfall of the private property and wage systems.[1] Communists aim to lead the revolution and to command the new socialist world order by having charge of the "dictatorship of the proletariat" by which it is to be ruled.[2]

The chief instrument to carry out this mission is the Communist Party with branches in all countries and its headquarters now in Moscow. But it is not a political party in the ordinary sense. It is not intended to be a voting aggregation, to gain power by legal means, but rather a thoroughly trained, highly disciplined Military Staff and vanguard of the revolutionary masses to seize power by violence and to hold it by terror, "unlimited power, resting on violence and not on law." In the words of Lenin, as quoted by Stalin:

> The successful victory over capitalism requires a correct relationship between the leading Communist Party and the revolutionary class, the proletariat, on the one hand, and the masses, i.e., all those who toil and are exploited, on the other. Only the Communist Party, if it really is the vanguard of the revolutionary class, if it incorporates all the best representatives of the class, if it is composed of fully conscious and devoted Communists who have been educated and steeled by the experience of stubborn revolutionary struggle, if this party has succeeded in linking itself inseparably with the whole life of its class

> and through this class with the whole mass of the exploited, and in imbuing this class and these masses with complete confidence – only such a party is capable of leading the proletariat in the most ruthless, decisive, and final struggle against all the forces of capitalism.[3]

The proselytizing power of the Party arises primarily from mass discontent with the existing order to which Communists attribute all the annoyances and troubles of life. The Party takes full advantage of the many admitted defects of the present system, a large part of which are rooted in human nature itself and would be present under any arrangement. It thrives on such things as the failure of classical political economy to explain or mitigate business crises; the inadequacies and the distortions of orthodox history; the failure of church and other leaders to recognize and face the great issues of our times; the universal tendency to envy those who are better off and to blame "the system" for personal failure and maladjustment; the secret desire to witness, perhaps aid, the downfall of those in superior positions gained, it is supposed, by foul play or personal connections, rather than merit. Finally, there is the idealistic attraction of the slogan "from each according to his ability and to each according to his need." The prospect offered seems like perfect brotherhood and altruistic interest in the welfare of one's fellow men, which contrasts sharply with the cold, self-regarding character of private enterprise. But those who permit themselves to follow this lure fail to realize what Russia has learned, though she does not preach it, namely, that in practice removal of incentive for superior performance provided by personal reward in accordance with deed causes interest and performance to fall, and compulsion, by enslavement or worse, to follow.

The first country to fall to world communism was Russia, which since the Bolshevist Revolution of October, 1917, has provided a powerful national base for international communist operations. A strong effort is now made to create the impression that the Communist International has been dissolved, that there is no longer any connection between Russia and communist parties in other countries. Stalin when recently asked, "What is your opinion regarding the accusation that the policies of communist parties in western Europe are 'dictated by Moscow'?" replied, "I consider the accusation absurd and to be borrowed from the bankrupt arsenal of Hitler and Goebbels."[4]

Yet in his own book, *Problems of Leninism*, currently revised by him, translated under his authorization into all civilized languages, distributed by communist parties everywhere, and accepted by them as unquestionable gospel, Stalin cries: "For what else is our country, the country that is building socialism, if not the base of the world revolution?"[5] Quoting Lenin, he says:

> The victory of socialism is possible, first in a few or even in one single capitalist country taken separately. The victorious proletariat of that country, having expropriated the capitalists and organized its own socialist production, would rise against the rest of the capitalist world, attract to itself the oppressed classes of other countries, raise revolts among them against the capitalists, and even in the event of necessity come out even with armed forces against the exploiting classes and their states.[6]
>
> It is inconceivable that the Soviet republic should continue to exist for a long period side by side with imperialist states. Ultimately one or the other must conquer. Meanwhile a number of terrible clashes between the Soviet republic and the bourgeois states in inevitable. This means that if the proletariat, as the ruling class, wants to and will rule, it must prove it also by military organization.[7]

Stalin says that all but traitors to the cause of communism must accept these views, that to deny them "is to abandon internationalism, to abandon Leninism."[8] In his equally widely translated and distributed *Foundations of Leninsm*, Stalin says:

> But overthrowing the power of the bourgeoisie and establishing the power of the proletariat in a single country does not yet guarantee the complete victory of socialism. After consolidating its power and leading the peasantry after it, the proletariat of the victorious country can and must build up socialist society. But does that mean that in this way the proletariat will secure a complete and final victory for socialism, i.e., does it mean that with the forces of a single country it can finally consolidate socialism and fully guarantee that country against intervention, which means against restoration? Certainly not. That requires victory for the revolution in at least several countries. It is therefore the essential task of the victorious revolution in one country to develop and support the revolution in others. So the revolution in a victorious country ought not consider itself as a self-contained unit, but as an auxiliary and a means of hastening the victory of the proletariat in other countries.

> Lenin has tersely expressed this thought by saying that the task of the victorious revolution is to do the "utmost possible in one country for the development, support and stirring up of the revolution *in all countries*."[9]

In the same work, Stalin emphasizes the necessity of maintaining absolute uniformity of policy in all branches of the world communist party through iron discipline.[10] He says:

> But the parties of the Communist International, which organize their activities on the basis of the task of achieving and strengthening the dictatorship of the proletariat, cannot afford to be "liberal" or to permit the formation of factions. The Party is synonymous with unity of will, which leaves no room for factionalism or division of authority in the Party.[11]

This is the reason for the well-known close conformity of the American Communist Party to Moscow policy. And neither these realities nor the quotations just given can be obliterated for Mr. Stalin's present convenience as absurdities "borrowed from the bankrupt arsenal of Hitler and Goebbels." Lying and deception are among communism's most useful weapons. Stalin explains the necessity of deceiving one's bourgeois enemies, even when serving as allies, of waging relentless war against all bourgeois states, *i.e.*, states operating under the private property system, which includes the United States of America. Quoting Lenin, he says:

> To carry on a war for the overthrow of the international bourgeoisie, which is a hundred times more difficult, prolonged and complicated than the most stubborn of ordinary wars between states; and to refuse beforehand to maneuver, to utilize the conflict of interests (even though temporary) among one's enemies; to refuse to temporise and compromise with possible (even though transient, unstable, vacillating and conditional) allies—is not this ridiculous in the extreme? Is it not as though, in the difficult ascent of an unexplored and hitherto inaccessible mountain, we were to renounce beforehand the idea that at all times we might have to go in zigzags, sometimes retracing our steps, sometimes giving up the course once selected and trying various others.?[12]

Russia's wartime pretense that she had abandoned the revolution both at home and abroad was done merely to deceive her unstable allies of the moment, was merely a necessary zig-zag or strategic retreat in the continuing effort to reach the ultimate goal of destruction of private enterprise throughout the world. In a speech to the Russian people, February 9, 1946, Stalin made clear that the Kremlin looks upon the Soviet Union as its own united nations organization which it wishes to spread all over the world ostensibly to end wars and other difficulties among nations. He said:

> The Soviet state system has proved an example of a multinational state system where the national problem and the problem of collaboration among nations are solved better than in any other multinational state.[12A]

While assuring the Russians that under normal conditions they are better off than any other people, the Kremlin constantly paints the outside world in lurid, hateful colors. It tells the people that the diabolical capitalists are plotting to attack them from within and from without in order to destroy the workers' paradise which threatens to overthrow the capitalist system of exploitation. Stalin in 1939, for example, warned the Communist Party:

> Never to forget that we are surrounded by a capitalist world; to remember that the foreign espionage services will smuggle spies, murderers and wreckers into our country; and, remembering this, to strengthen our socialist intelligence service and systematically help it to defeat and eradicate the enemies of the people.[13]

A people thus stirred up to believe they are fighting to save their national life are more easily ruled, more willing to obey orders unquestioningly, more willing to accept purges of their ranks as necessary cleansings of deadly capitalistic influences. Any Russian found conversing with a foreigner is naturally suspected of being an agent of free enterprise and is dealt with accordingly.

Between those who accept and those who reject the teachings of communist ideology and the decrees of its leaders there is and can be no compromise, no give and take, no margin of tolerance. When they get the upper hand, Communists root out and destroy under a reign of terror all capitalistic elements and influences. They believe that the workers as they are awakened to the truth about their former masters will welcome the new order as a vast improvement over the old. Lenin said, as quoted by Stalin:

> The dictatorship of the proletariat . . . is not merely the use of violence against the exploiters, and is not even mainly the use of violence. The economic basis of this revolutionary violence, the

> guarantee of its vitality and success, is that the proletariat represents and introduces a higher type of social organization of labor compared with capitalism. That is the essential point. This is the source of the strength of Communism and the guarantee of its inevitable complete victory.[14]

The German Program

Communists believe that fascism is the final state of capitalism, that when it falls, as it must, it can be succeeded only by communism.[15] They believe that our attempt to democratize fascist Germany in the western sense is as futile as to try to transform a chicken into an egg or a butterfly into a larva. They believe that Germany must pass through a natural metamorphosis from nazism to communism, and that when they help the process along they are working in harmony with the inevitable course of history.

Walther Ulbricht, Director of the Communist Party in Germany, whose wife was a secretary to General Zhukov, and who was in Russia between 1933 and V-E Day, stated before a secret Berlin meeting of the "Free German Trade Union's" 45-man executive committee for the Soviet zone:

> When the job of Communizing the Soviet zone is completed we shall devote ourselves to the other zones.
>
> Soon there will not be any privately owned companies in the Soviet zone in Germany. All the large companies, even medium-sized ones will revert to community ownership. This must be done rapidly, before the establishment of a central administration in Germany can interfere in our zone.[16]

Communism is fundamentally an attack against private property and the propertied class. In the Russian zone the process of stripping Germans of their property has been accomplished by destruction through war action, by looting, reparations, inflation, confiscation, and by forced sales. Meanwhile, liquidation of the property owning classes has been completed by denazification, forced labor, executions, and terror which has led thousands to suicide and other thousands to turn fugitive and thus to forfeit their holdings.

We have already noted the thoroughness with which the zone was sacked and looted, yielding billions of dollars worth of lucre to Russia. The other operations have been equally devastating.

Inflation, which destroys whole classes and eats the very marrow out of the bones of any economy, has been deliberately created. Russia's share of the occupation marks which had been printed up in advance by the U.S. Treasury was not enough. She asked for the plates and after we turned them over to her printed up and circulated untold billions more. Finally, she opened the vaults of the Reichsbank, its branches, and other banks and seized their contents.[17] The resulting inflation has yielded fabulous spoil at little or no cost and as the same time helped to ruin and expropriate the propertied class.

The dispossessed German masses have been reduced to prostrate, helpless, submissive proletarians. Having lost all individual security, they are utterly dependent upon their new masters for jobs, food, and all other necessities. Since nothing is supplied to critics and objectors, survivors are submissive. Farmers, as stated before, were stripped of equipment, tools, seeds, and livestock during the early looting. To obtain replacements necessary to carry on operations they must apply to the "co-operatives" which are under communist control and which use their monopoly to prevent "politically unreliable" farmers from obtaining essential supplies. Unless they submit, they must abandon farming and give up their land. In this fashion the way is opened wide for zonal sovietization with minimum interference.[18]

Soviet authorities believe that the German masses will enthusiastically accept the liquidation of the propertied classes as liberation from capitalistic exploitation. Carefully censored press and radio assure them that the present painful difficulties are only birth pains of a glorious new order which had been blocked by the former upper classes. In harmony with this thought, all schools and universities that are operating teach the Germans the advantages of communism and belittle the western democracies as strongholds of fascism and capitalistic exploitation, of wretched imperialism and fomenters of imperialist wars. Such ideas are taught the members of the Russian sponsored, nationwide "Free Youth" movement,[19] and thousands of children who have been snatched from their families and placed in special children's "Homes" for systematic indoctrination.[20] Here is a sample of what they are taught:

> In comparison with the Soviet Republic, the parliamentarian democracies are a step backward . . . The difference between bourgeois society in the Soviet Union is like the difference between ape and man. Socialism is the future of all humanity . . . The old powers can delay this development, but they cannot destroy it . . . This change in the structure of society cannot be achieved in a reformatory way. You can only achieve it in the revolutionary way . . . If this socialist structure we have in Russia were introduced in all nations of the world, it would be impossible to wage war, just as war is impossible between the Ukraine and Armenia.[21]

The Soviets, according to their lights, are making an effort to woo the Germans into acceptance of communism and to minimize resentment. As already noted, they have handled denazification with comparative enlightenment. Scientists, technologists, military experts, and others with special talents have been eagerly sought after and offered attractive inducements to render service to the new regime. Penitent nazis are invited to transfer allegiance to the Communist Party and to start working through it for German salvation. Taking advantage of the deep resentment of the French and Morgenthau proposals to amputate the western Reich, Communists have taken the lead in an intensely pro-Fatherland movement. This gives the Germans the impression that the western democracies who would stand in the way of "the new and greater German Reich" are the real enemies, rather than either nazism or communism.[22] Russian occupation troops apparently no longer molest frauleins, "at least not in the careless, irresponsible way the Americans do," reports an American correspondent.[23] It is interesting to note in this connection that only one man remains in the zone for every 15 women in the 20 to 30 years of age bracket.[24]

Hitler had freed the peasants of the scourge of usurious mortgage holders; Russia goes a step further in her bid for popular approval by breaking up the Junker and other large estates and making the land available in small plots of between 11 and 17 acres to approved Germans on easy terms.[25] The operation does not increase total production but appears to spread ownership. The maneuver is obviously a preliminary to collectivization similar to the procedure followed in liquidation of the Ukrainian Kulaks. The new "owners" are promised houses and equipment. Since these are not available, the owners have no choice but to band together in the existing estate buildings, where collectivist headquarters must be located. Collectivization can thus proceed a little later with minimum disturbance, and the new government can with ease slip into position to exploit those who work the soil in place of the former owners.

All farmers are given production quotas to fill at controlled prices. Part of any surplus, and there rarely is one since the quotas are set so high, may be sold in markets where those with the money to buy, usually members of the new ruling bureaucracy, can buy food to supplement rations, which are nominally set at about the same level as those in the American zone. The requisite supplies are not always available in many places, however, and widespread starvation has occurred.[26] Persistent reports nevertheless tell of substantial food exports to Russia.[27] However, people are allowed rationed brown coal for residential heating,[28] whereas, as previously mentioned, Berliners and those in the western zone have had no coal to heat their homes.

The industries left in the zone are all in operation and are either managed by Russians or "workers' councils" dominated by Communists. Although most of the product is taken as reparation and sent to the Soviet Union, a small amount is made available for sale to the German workers. Correspondents permitted to tour the zone in March, 1946, reported that a long list of manufactured products were on display, including carpenter tools, typewriters, sewing machines, even automobiles.[29] They reported that the Germans they saw displayed less of an attitude of futility and a more vigorous spirit than are encountered in other zones.[30]

Only one political party is allowed, the Social Unity Party, representing a forced merger of the Communist and Social Democratic Parties, with the former completely dominant. Since all positions carrying power, prestige, and higher than ordinary incomes are held by Communists and their pets, thousands of Germans have rushed into the Party simply to gain its perquisites.[31] The Germans are learning spoils politics from their Red overlords on a scale that would make a Tammany ward heeler blush.[32] Even if Russia should be forced to withdraw her occupation forces with political control returned to the Germans, the deeply entrenched German Communists would no doubt continue to maintain themselves in power and in all probability provide the whole of Germany with political leadership.[33]

The way for ultimate communization of the western areas is being assiduously prepared by Communists in the western zones of occupation,[34] many of whom have worked their way into important posts in both the occupation bureaucracies and the local governmental establishments which have been set up to be run by Germans under the watchful eye of the military forces. Such communist penetration has automatically been abetted by the Potsdam program, by deindustrialization, denazification, enslavement, repression, by the whole terrible catastrophe. The roaming bands of vagabonds may be a curse to the western zonal authorities, but they afford the Communists excellent revolutionary material. Since the institution of private property and the propertied classes are now largely wiped out, the way has been opened for converting the whole Reich into a Sovietized "democracy."

We have done much already to facilitate realization of Russia's plans, and the Kremlin expects us to do more. It wants us to accept the Russian claim to 10 billion dollars in German reparations, not only to produce handsome booty but to place such a load on the crippled German economy that it could survive only under communization.[35] It is to Russia's advantage to delay the signing of a peace treaty with Germany as long as possible, for the delay will give her plans that much longer to mature. And if any German government is to be set up in the meantime, Russia wants it to be a provisional, centralized government, one that will give maximum opportunity to the thoroughly entrenched Communists to draw into their grasp controls over all of Germany.

The West Awakens

The West has been slow to recognize that the Russian ally is really no ally at all, but a determined enemy, that behind the Kremlin's every move lurks a sinister, dangerous motive. Our own leaders were long caught under the influence of Mr. Roosevelt's "great design," the strategy of trying to cure the Soviet leaders of their suspicion, animosity, and hatred of the West by showering them with favors and kindness. While under the spell we considered the truculent sons of Russia prodigals just returning to the family of nations, and felt it our duty to cater to their whims and eccentricities, to overlook their insults and stabs.

We signed the Potsdam Declaration, without suspecting that it was a Russian booby trap, that its vague, contradictory, undefined provisions and phrases could be applied by and yield advantage to only a Soviet Union which thrives on human misery. We shut our eyes to the vital difference between our way of life and Russian communism. Because Communists called their way "democracy," we assumed it was somehow akin to our "democracy" and we accepted in good faith Russia's wartime pretension that she was finished with revolution both at home and abroad, that her aggressions were nothing more than moves to strengthen her "essential security."

We have had our clashes with the Russians both in and out of Germany, have endured slaps and humiliations such as Americans have never accepted before. We have permitted our telephone lines running through the Russian zone to our zone in Berlin to be tapped. We have even put up with a Russian refusal to supply our Berlin zone with fresh food. We have bowed to Russian refusal to permit us to double track our single rail line into Berlin. We have had serious conflicts over newspaper censorship, control of radio outlets and programs, schools and school curricula, and a multitude of things both important and trivial, taking it all with a friendly smile when we had to yield to Soviet demands.

But finally we began to realize that such tactics were impressing the Russians only as weakness and to awaken to the menacing character of Soviet designs. Mildly at first, but with growing determination, we began to take a firmer stand, to demand that our own interests be given some attention. Our disillusionment was complete when Mr. Molotov at Paris finally showed his hand. We have been staggering to our senses ever since. We must hope that the awakening has come in time to prevent the Kremlin from absorbing the German Reich.

In the struggle we must recognize that Russia will have certain advantages, apart from those gained by our attempt to apply the sadistic Potsdam decrees, including deep German resentment. The Russian bureaucracy with its long experience in managing economic institutions and processes had found it relatively simple to take over control of the German economy in its zone and is fully prepared to extend the control over the rest of the Reich when opportunity presents itself. On the other hand, our own Government and especially our military forces are notoriously incompetent in handling economic affairs. Conditions reached bottom early in the Russian zone, so that what change has come has been for the better; whereas, bad as things are in our zone, they must be expected to become progressively worse. Germans will not fail to note the contrast and to draw dangerous conclusions. As stated before, the former movement of Germans from the East to the West has already reversed. Thousands of disillusioned, discouraged Germans are crossing into the Russian zone where they will enthusiastically prepare to help drive the hateful democracies out of Germany.

We have numerous advantages, however, which, if handled properly, should prove decisive. German antipathy toward Russia and Bolshevism is deepseated; in contrast, Germans have hitherto always admired us Americans and have imitated us in many ways, especially in economic techniques. Russia has also compromised herself in fundamental ways. She was behind the terrible expulsions of Germans from the lost territories and other places. She has been the instigator and chief beneficiary of the same system, having taken from three to four times as many prisoners as all the western powers together. Germans of all classes deeply resent the cruel and violent liquidation of the former upper and middle classes, especially because it was carried out by foreigners and Communists whose patriotism is suspect.

Our task is to formulate a new and just German peace program—one that will give effect to our basic ideals and convictions and lead Germany toward, not away from, us and our way of life. But before we can take this step intelligently we must first face certain basic facts, must disabuse our minds of certain gross misconceptions which have lowered us in German esteem and misled us into the present danger.

CHAPTER TEN

Facts We Must Face

How We Have Played into Russia's Hands

General Eisenhower told a press conference in London that the Russians "like to laugh." Well they might, in view of the way we have played into their hands and fallen for their subterfuges.

Things have come to such a pass that we have seriously been told we must not criticize the Russians or their government; yet those who said so have felt perfectly free to criticize everything American and have made no corresponding effort to stop Soviet blasts at us.

In March, 1945, GIs in Germany were actually placed under official orders not to make unflattering remarks about the Reds.[1] Typical of our un-American efforts to throttle critics was AMG censorship in April, 1946, of a letter by a Catholic Bishop calling attention to Russian abuses of Germans through forced labor and expulsions. We prohibited the reading of the letter in churches, because it might offend Russia.[2] Social Democrats and other German political parties have not been allowed to criticize the Communist party, lest Russia take offense.

We must realize that there is something seriously wrong with nations, as with people, who cannot stand criticism, who try to place themselves beyond reproach, and that something is equally wrong with people who truckle to them.

Russia deserves not only criticism but condemnation. Stalin in 1939 told the Communist Party of Russia it must beware of us, for we would send our "spies, murderers, and wreckers" into the Soviet Union. The facts are that the Soviet Union has sent its spies, murderers, and wreckers into this country, as in all others, where they have infiltrated into our government, occupying hundreds of key positions, sitting in our inner councils, and even helping mold our foreign policy.

It must make the Russians chortle up their sleeves the way we coddle these insidious fifth columnists. In contrast, the Reds shoot on suspicion anyone they catch in Russia who they think might represent outside influences.

In the Canadian spy trial it was established both by direct testimony and documentary proof that "the dissolution of the Communist International was probably the greatest farce of the Communists in recent years," and that "only the name was liquidated with the object of reassuring public opinion in the democratic countries. Actually, the Comintern exists and continues its work." Communist insiders were warned by their higher-ups with regard to Britain and the United States: "Yesterday they were allies, today they are neighbors, tomorrow they will be our enemies." It was also brought out that "in Russia there is a great deal of propaganda carried on by conversation of the propagandists and even in the press. It is all done to train people to think they must fight another war, that maybe it will be our final war."[3]

In Germany we have permitted the Comintern to place its agents in AMG and the local German government apparatus we have erected. Newspapermen in our zone tend to lean toward communism, mostly because former anti-Nazi talent was first cleared for press work by German emigres with leftist leanings hired by AMG to do the screening.[4]

In May, 1946, it was revealed that the State Department with the aid of the FBI had purged itself of hundreds of pro-Soviet employees.[5] Some time later Mr. Byrnes, head of the department, when asked why certain others had not been let out, despite their having been identified, replied that it would be inadvisable to do so while we are involved in a serious diplomatic struggle with the Soviet Union.[6]

His excuse was a tacit admission that he recognized that the men are agents of the Soviet Government, and that the Kremlin might get upset if we turned the rotters out.

There is no valid reason why we should treat Russia and her fifth column any differently from the way we treated Nazi Germany and its fifth column. The only important difference between the two in terms of their threat against our national tranquility and safety is that the Soviet fifth column is far stronger and more deeply entrenched than the Nazi one ever was. If it was right for us to crack down on the Nazis here the way we did, without regard to Hitler's feelings, it is right that we should crack down with equal firmness and effectiveness on the Communists in our midst, without regard to Stalin's feelings, for all of them would be potential traitors and saboteurs if we should get into serious trouble with Russia.

One of the most costly consequences of Soviet penetration of our State Department has been our acceptance of wily Russian proposals at Yalta and Potsdam. These include: division of Germany into zones, each to be occupied by a different power; the allied Control Council, with the clause calling for unanimity on all decisions, with the disastrous results already noted; requiring Germany to pay reparations in kind; the forced labor system; the forcible expulsions of Germans from lost German territories, Poland, Hungary, and Czechoslovakia. The territorial settlements and arrangements accepted at Potsdam, were all the ones pressed by Russia; French claims were left open. The idea of a long armistice for Germany, if not of actual Russian origin, would certainly play into Russia's hands.[7]

Britain and the United States in the days between Teheran and Potsdam, thanks in large measure to Mr. Roosevelt's unfortunate "great design" and Red influences in the administration, were eager to borrow any Soviet idea and acclaim any Soviet plan for Germany. Although deeply involved in war, the brains of the Politburo found the time to frame a program to take full advantage of the westerners' solicitude. They have been cashing in on it ever since, and we have been suffering the consequences.

We have even given Russia help both direct and indirect in extending her power over eastern Europe and half of Germany. Instead of following Churchill's advice of attacking Germany through the Balkans and thus warding off Russian conquest and occupation, we sided with Russia and decided to attack across the English Channel. As the Russians swept into the Balkans and on into Austria and Germany, they rode in American lend-lease trucks, jeeps and airplanes. Since then we have supported their brutal rule through such agencies as UNRRA. As fast as we have shipped relief supplies into these areas, Russia has drained out an equivalent amount for herself and claims the credit for what we pour in.[8] In Germany we even handed the Russians our money plates and permitted them to print billions of occupation marks which we were originally supposed to make good, and possibly still are. But all such aid, including the eleven billion dollars in lend-lease gifts has been ignored by the Kremlin which has gone blithely on its way opposing our most vital interests.

We Should Have Known Better

In addition to all this, as Dorothey Thompson has well expressed it: "Mr. Morgenthau's fantastic concepts laid the basic 'principles' for the Potsdam program, which played straight into Soviet hands."[9] In other words, the Morgenthau Plan was made to order for the Kremlin.

When we came to Russia at Yalta with a so-called peace plan which called for vengeance and destruction of a trade competitor, she saw and seized her opportunity to turn the whole program to her advantage at our expense.

Although the Plan promises to bring the blessings of peace and prosperity to a troubled world, if we had only taken the trouble to analyze its proposals in the light of Mr. Morgenthau's own principles as expressed in other connections on other occasions, we should have recognized immediately that it could only bring catastrophe.

In promoting acceptance of the Bretton Woods Fund and Bank Plan, Mr. Morgenthau as Secretary of the Treasury, proclaimed the thesis that "prosperity, like peace, is indivisible." And in promoting the loan to Britain later on he elaborated at length on this principle. These are his words:

> If we have learned nothing else from the frightful experience of war, we should have learned at least that we live in an *incorrigibly integrated world.* It is a world which cannot exist half slave and half free, nor half at war and half at peace. Neither can it exist half prosperous and half impoverished. Prosperity, like peace is indivisible. *It must be shared by all if any are to enjoy it.* Our own living standards cannot rise and remain at high levels without *progressive prosperity throughout the world.* As I have observed before, prosperity cannot be segmented; *all* must share in it or in time *all* will lose it.[10] (emphasis added)

The contradiction between these tenets and the deliberate impoverishment of any nation is irreconcilable and obvious. Mr. Morgenthau advances these ideas as universal principles, applicable to all countries without exception. If they could validly be used to support making sacrifices to put one country, Britain, on its feet to bolster world peace and prosperity, with equal force they compel the conclusion that a program calling for permanent impoverishment of any leading country, Germany not excepted, would plunge the whole world into an economic quagmire.

Mr. Morgenthau is not alone, however, in thus compromising himself with his own principles. Mr. Bernard Baruch, well known adviser of Presidents, has also been at one and the same time a one-worlder and an implacable advocate of converting Germany into a poor house. As the war was drawing to its close in the European theater, Mr. Baruch, who loves to address his audiences as "Fellow citizens of the world," was in London where he granted an interview to A. Victor Lasky, a *Stars and Stripes* staff writer. In explaining his presence in the British capital, Baruch said, according to Lasky:

> And one reason I am over here is to hold a big stick over the big boys to make damn sure they're not going to foul up the peace. We've got to de-industrialize Germany and Japan—for at least a generation—to see that those subsidized slave labor countries do not again flood the world with their cheap products . . .[11]

This was Mr. Baruch's way of saying that he was abroad to see to it that Germany was permanently eliminated as a competitor in world trade.

Baruch failed to explain the nature of the "big stick" he was holding over the big boys, but the following June, before the Senate Military Affairs Committee, he made very clear what he wanted done with the Reich. He said it was not enough merely to demand an "economically weak" Germany, that the program of weakening Germany must be "sufficiently specific—industry by industry—so that all the occupying nations know they have agreed to the same thing." First of all, he said, reparations should be paid in German labor, instead of rebuilding the country's industry so it could pay reparations through exports from current production. Germany's "war making potential must be eliminated. Many of her plants must be shifted east and west to friendly countries; all heavy industries destroyed; the Junker estates broken up; her exports strictly controlled; German assets and business organizations all over the world rooted out."

This program of impoverishment and that of Mr. Morgenthau are, of course, very similar. Mr. Baruch candidly admits that his aim is to destroy Germany as a trade competitor; Mr. Morgenthau's program tacitly contains the same objective. People were appalled when it was said that the elder Rockefeller burned down the refineries of competitors he could not otherwise destroy. How much more revolting are these proposals to destroy the economy of a whole nation for a similar purpose! Conservative leaders who use their influence in this manner furnish a basis for effective criticism of capitalistic morality, or lack of it, and weaken the basis for defense of the profit system. Since, according to the one world thesis, prosperity "must be shared by all if any are to enjoy it," and "all must share in it or in time all will lose it," the Morgenthau-Baruch Plan would impoverish not only Germany, but Europe, and the whole world, not excluding the United States, and therefore presumably Messrs. Baruch and Morgenthau as well.

The Morgenthau-Baruch proposals have been the official policy of our Government, which at the same time is committed to one-world principles. As a result, our leading officials, in their efforts to uphold these mutually exclusive theories, have been forced, like Mr. Morgenthau, into absurd self-contradiction. For example, Mr. Truman, while advocating impoverishment of Germany along Morgenthau-Baruch lines, said at Soldiers Field in Chicago:

> We shall work to achieve equal opportunity in world trade because closed economic blocs in Europe or *any place in the world* can only lead to impoverishment and isolation of the people who inhabit it. We shall press for the elimination of artificial barriers to international navigation, in order that *no nation*, by accident of geographic location, shall be denied unrestricted access to seaports and international waterways.

Later he said in the same speech:

> Economic distress, *anywhere in the world*, is a fertile breeding ground for violent political upheaval.[12]

By continuing our policy of creating economic distress in Germany, we would therefore create a fertile breeding ground for communism. Here, Mr. Truman admits as much.

In his speech in Stuttgart, Mr. Byrnes contradicted himself in similar fashion, for he tried to justify the original program of deindustrialization and denazification, which means holding Germany in poverty, and at the same time said:

> We have learned, whether we like it or not, that we live in *one world* from which we cannot isolate ourselves. We have learned that *peace and well-being are indivisible.*

Before we can win the respect of the world and get on the right road leading to real world prosperity and well-being, we must eradicate the whole Morgenthau and Potsdam contamination from our thinking and official policies.

Germany, the Heart of Europe

We must take seriously the recognized fact that Germany is the heart of Europe on which the economic life of that Continent depends, and that when we make that heart stop beating all Europe must die. We must realize, too, that any reduction of the German standard of living would only lower the standards of other European countries, that to bring them all to the same mean level would bring universal impoverishment that would cancel out the progress of centuries.

Despite his one-world principles expressed elsewhere, Mr. Morgenthau in his book, *Germany is Our Problem*, writes:

> Actually there is no "European Economy," certainly not in the sense that there is a United States economy. Some thirty countries in Europe have their separate economies, and a great variety of them, too. (p. 31)

He factiously argues that "a strong Europe is better than a strong Germany," as though the two were opposed, and insists that weakening Germany and reducing her foreign trade will add to European prosperity. He says:

> Before World War I, Germany accounted for 12 per cent of the world's international commerce. By the 1920's her share had fallen below 10 per cent. In 1936 and 1937 it was a bit more than 8 per cent. The world would not be the loser if Germany fell to 2 or 3 per cent and her share were taken over by other nations. (pp. 71-2)

In short, where Germany is concerned, Mr. Morgenthau finds foreign trade quite unimportant either for the Reich or for the countries trading with her; however, when other countries are involved, foreign trade takes on unique importance.

In a statement submitted to the Small Business Committee of the Senate, April 20, 1945, Mr. Morgenthau said:

> Our exports may seem to be only a small part of our total production. They are, nevertheless, vital . . . They mean the difference between prosperity and depression for both agriculture and industry.

On Feb. 26, 1945, he told the Detroit Economic Club, while urging building up our exports of automobiles to a million cars a year:

> We can reach such a trade level only if both the producing and consuming powers of *all countries* are expanded, not merely restored to their old levels.

Such statements show that Mr. Morgenthau himself, if he will only think things through, must repudiate his proposals to impoverish the Reich and destroy its trade with the rest of the world, or give up one-world principles.

Britain's experience testifies eloquently to the importance of Germany to European economy. At first she fell under the influence of those advocating German impoverishment, ostensibly to prevent another war but actually to remove the Reich as a trade competitor and possibly turn it into a market for the very products it had formerly exported. But when she saw that Germany was facing complete disaster, and pulling Europe down with her, she partly reversed her position, to prevent what "approximated closely to cutting off one's nose to spite one's face." For, after all, she had to realize that destruction of Germany to prevent German exports from competing with hers would also mean loss of a large German demand for British goods. As Prime Minister Attlee told the U.S. Congress, "We cannot have prosperity at home with hell abroad."

The German prostration has been felt everywhere. Sweden has officially expressed concern over the fact that she has been unable to carry on any of her accustomed trade with the Reich, with damaging consequences to herself as well as to Germany.[13] Holland, too, has been hard hit, having to export food and fuel while the homeland does without. Dutch farmers used to exchange food products for German fertilizer, which they can obtain now only at high prices from high cost producers. Holland used to get fees for transmitting goods between Germany and other countries;

now this trade and its profit are gone with the suppression of German commerce. Germany and Holland used to exchange the things each made best in its own country. This put German machinery, tools, and instruments in Dutch plants, on Dutch farms and railroads. Now this equipment cannot be replaced or even repaired due to stoppage of manufacture in the Reich. As one observer puts it:

> The deindustrialization decrees have been encouraged by less efficient interests of the United Nations, especially England, which hope to gain by the death sentences for German competition. The Netherlands and other countries are missing what they used to get from Germany.[14]

In London, "Food ministers of 17 European countries," says an Associated Press dispatch, "turned to defeated Germany as a possible source of coal and fertilizer, both sorely needed to avoid famine."[15]

Showing deep concern, the *London Economist* says:

> The truth is that the prosperity of Western Europe has depended to a great extent upon the existence of a great wealth producing industrial concentration in the Ruhr. That wealth-producing machinery is now almost completely idle, and all of Germany's western neighbors are bearing the consequences.
>
> To say that the ruin of Germany is the ruin of Europe would not raise in Russia more than a sigh of relief that both should be weakened together. The American attitude is more difficult to understand.[16]

The *Chicago Sun* said editorially:

> It is good business—plain, hardboiled common sense—for any wholesaler to help his best customer back on his feet when that customer is in financial difficulty. If the customer is a whole nation, the need becomes immensely more pressing.[17]

Of course this was said in defense of a loan to Britain, but the same logic would apply as well to Germany, once one of our best customers.

Mr. Byrnes said at Paris: "The economic revival of Germany is essential to the well-being of Europe."

At Stuttgart he admitted, as had Molotov at Paris, that Germany is the industrial workshop of Europe.

To repeat, we are having to face the fact that we cannot continue with our original policies toward Germany and hope to have anything but impoverishment of Germany, and, as a consequence, of Europe, and the world.

The Matter of War Guilt

Mr. Morgenthau, whose ideas on the subject correspond to the official opinion of the United Nations, rests his entire case for turning Germany into a poorhouse on the thesis that German lust for war was the *sole* cause of both World Wars. "Desire for war," he writes in his book, "has been as firmly planned in the German as desire for freedom in the American." Sheer will to war, accompanied by a plot to conquer the world, he says, has been intensively cultivated in the German people for nearly two hundred years and would probably require another two hundred years to eradicate. Hence, he argues, the only way to stop Germany from again disturbing the peace of the world at her first opportunity is to prevent the opportunity, and this can be done best by permanently weakening her to a point where she cannot, even though she would, wage war.[18]

The justice of his whole program, and therefore of Potsdam, must stand or fall on this premise. If there is any doubt as to its validity or completeness, there must be equal doubt as to the justice of his plan.

Without attempting to exhaust the subject we offer the following evidence which does tend to raise doubt concerning to accuracy of the premise, and therefore equal doubt as to the justice of our treatment of the German people.

Let us again consult Mr. Morgenthau on other occasions. On March 7, 1945, he told the House Committee on Banking and Currency:

> Power politics . . . has become a term of reproach in the world . . . The United Nations hope to abolish it from the earth. But power economics may be just as dangerous, for if it is not the root of all evil in international affairs it is at the very least a frequent cause of conflict. The legislation before this committee is our best hope of banishing that too.
>
> We cannot say that we will join the other nations in an organization to maintain peace, but will not help remove *one of the most dangerous causes of war—economic dislocation.*[19]

Economic dislocation is hardly the same thing as the perversity of German nature of "will to war."

Three months later, Mr. Morgenthau told the Senate Banking and Currency Committee:

> Peace is more than a political problem. It is a complicated structure that can be built only upon the solid foundation of *economic order and prosperity in all countries*. Peace and prosperity are two sides of the same problem. We can't neglect one without endangering the other. If peace is to endure, there must be jobs, there must be *hope of economic betterment*.
>
> International monetary and financial problems have been *a source of conflict for a generation*. We must see that after this war they do not become the basis for new conflicts.[20]

Lack of prosperity and hope of economic betterment and international monetary and financial problems were therefore at least partly to blame for the recent war, according to Mr. Morgenthau himself, not merely German lust for war, argued in his book.

He told the St. Louis Chamber of Commerce:

> After the last war, informal attempts were made to stabilize currencies but they failed . . . Competitive currency depreciation led to other forms of economic warfare . . . New currency tricks restricted and burdened trade. They must certainly be counted as a contributory cause of the great depression. And *they were the first phase of the tragic war in which we are now engaged.*[21]

Mr. Vinson, successor to Mr. Morgenthau as Secretary of the Treasury, gave his version of the causes of war in these words:

> We have the *political, social and economic problems* among nations that twice in our generation rocked us into war. The resolution of these problems is necessary for prolonged prosperity and for lasting peace.[22]

Solving such problems to prevent war is a far cry from our original policy of trying to maintain peace by turning Germany into a goat pasture.

Herbert E. Gaston, Assistant Secretary of the Treasury, in a published speech said:

> It was almost entirely because of the *sick condition of foreign trade* that we were barely getting out of the last depression when war came upon us.[23]

And on another occasion he said:

> It seemed even before the present war began with Germany's assault on Poland that *we could not have political peace without*

economic peace and that economic peace and thriving world trade were not possible except under conditions of monetary peace?[24]

That most wars, including the last one, have been caused by economic disruption and consequent "foul growths," to borrow a phrase from the late Lord Keynes, is a truism which no informed person will deny. Such dislocations and their results are not the same as human beings; human beings are the victims. Therefore, it is wrong to blame people for the forces which compel their behavior. When people fall into a trap where their very existence is threatened, they will fight their way out if there is any possiblity to do so. They will fight, even though it might appear suicidal to do so. For most people prefer to die fighting than to die supinely. Such behavior may be wrong, but it is the way people have behaved for many thousands of years, and the chances are that they will continue to do so.

The British themselves have often found conditions during peace more unbearable than war. Whenever the balance of power is upset in Europe so that the continent starts to fall under the domination of some one of its powers, Britain considers the situation a threat to her very existence and goes to war to preserve herself. One of the best and most authoritative analyses of the matter appeared in the September, 1943, issue of the semi-official British publication, *The Nineteenth Century and After* , by the editor, Mr. F.A. Voight. The following are pertinent excerpts:

> It is fashionable to dismiss the balance of power as an obsolete doctrine. It is not a doctrine. It is, for Great Britain and the Empire the immutable condition of survival. Any power that becomes undisputed master of the European mainland can become master of the British Isles . . .
>
> England has not one permanent foe in Europe, and none of her vital interests conflict with the vital interests of any European power. Her only foe is that power, or that coalition of powers, which may endeavor to dominate Europe. Against that foe she must always be ready, always be strong, and always have allies. As her foe varies, so her allies must vary. The foe of yesterday may be the ally of tomorrow and the ally of yesterday may be the foe of tomorrow:
>
> The power of the British Empire, plus the power of continental allies, will, if the Empire is strong, always balance the power of whatever power seeks domination. And as long as the balance is maintained, there will be peace, for no one power can prevail over

> the rest of Europe plus the British Empire, as long as the Empire is strong.
>
> This simple mechanism is the balance of power. It exists by virtue of the immutable physical realities. Neither the League of Nations, nor any system of collective security, nor disarmament can change these realities. As soon as the balance of power is challenged, every collective system will collapse and England will, if she is not to perish, make the counter-challenge. She did so in 1939. The mechanism of the balance was released and the League of Nations was at once deprived of whatever reality it had ever possessed on the 1st of September in that year, on the day when Germany attacked Poland and, so releasing the mechanism, began the Second World War. England fought to preserve the balance—for that reason and no other.
>
> The commonly accepted view that Germany made war to dominate the world is, in our opinion, mistaken.
>
> She wanted to be a world power, but world power and world domination are not the same thing (England is a world power, but she does not dominate the world). Hitler would have been glad to share the world with the English . . . Had England remained neutral he would have been successful. But she would then have been at his mercy, or the mercy of his successor—in any case at the mercy of the German Nation . . . Nothing could have saved England from destruction—except the good will of the Germans . . .
>
> It was to avert this fate that England went to war in 1939. It is to avert a similar fate in future years that the balance must always be maintained. The political complexion of those that maintain the balance is quite irrelevant . . . the nature of the peace must be determined by the enduring realities of the European situation, not by transient phenomena like fascism, national socialism, socialism, or communism. The exorbitant strength of Germany must be reduced and it must be kept reduced. Better a despotically governed Germany that is not too strong than a liberal Germany that is too strong . . . But it is . . . important that the weakening of Germany be relative rather than absolute.[25]

This explains in terms very different from Mr. Morgenthau's the underlying cause of the two world wars. It explains Britain's interest in the Potsdam agreements, including deindustrialization and denazification, and the exigencies behind Britain's present opposition to Russia, which again threatens to upset the European balance, just as Germany did. It disputes the thesis that the German people and their perversities were solely responsible for the war and should be punished accordingly.

It also clarifies a good many otherwise unexplained episodes connected with the war and its outbreak. It shows why Britain went to war ostensibly to oppose aggression, but applied the policy only to Germany, and not to Russia when she attacked Poland in full partnership with Germany. It explains the reason for the secret protocol attached to her declaration guaranteeing British and French aid to Poland, which qualified and limited the guarantee to *German* aggression and none other. The portion of this treaty that was made public at the time, gave the impression that the guarantee stood on moral ground, against any and all aggression. The published part stated:

> Should one of the contracting powers become engaged in hostilities with *a European power* in consequence of aggression by the latter against that contracting party, the other contracting party will at once give the contracting power engaged in hostilities all the support and assistance in its power.

Although the language is somewhat involved, the meaning is clear, that defense against aggression was the prime consideration and what England would fight for. The German attack against Poland was considered a high international wrong. But when Russia also attacked and Britain failed to oppose this aggression which was also a brutal stab in the back, but continued the war against Germany alone, it became clear to many observers that something more was present in the situation than readily met the eye. There was a *secret rider* attached to the treaty which has since been made public and which stipulates that "The expression, *a European power,* employed in the agreement is to be understood as *Germany.*"[26]

In other words, Britain was taking advantage of the situation to go to war against Germany because the Reich had become too strong and had upset the European balance. To correct the fundamental trouble, from Britain's point of view, Germany, after her defeat, must be weakened as a protective measure. No morality enters into the matter, only considerations of power politics and British survival.

Lord Lothian, then British ambassdor to the United States said in March, 1938, at the time of the Austrian crisis:

> If another war comes and the history of it is ever written, the dispassionate historian a hundred years hence, will say not that

Germany alone was responsible for it, even if she strikes first, but that those who mismanaged the world between 1918 and 1937 had a large share of responsibility in it.[27]

In his column, April 23, 1944, Karl Von Wiegand wrote:

> On April, 1939, four months before Hitler invaded Poland, Ambassador William C. Bullitt, whom I had known for 20 years, called me to the American embassy in Paris. Both of us standing before the fireplace in his office, the windows of which faced the beautiful Place de la Concorde, the American Ambassador told me that war had been decided upon. He did not say, nor did I ask, by whom. He let me infer it. When I said that in the end Germany would be driven into the arms of Soviet Russia and Bolshevism, the ambassador replied: "What of it. There will not be enough Germans left when the war is over to be worth Bolshevizing."[28]

A month earlier, according to the Associated Press:

> Joseph Stalin, in one of his most outspoken statements, told the world that Soviet Russia wouldn't be dragged into conflict with Germany as a "cat's paw" to pull British and French chestnuts out of the fire . . . Underlying the policy of nonintervention (against fascism) he said was a desire to embroil Italy, Japan, and Germany as deeply as possible in war against the Soviet Union and then, when they all had become weakened by conflict, "come on the stage with fresh forces" and dictate peace.[29]

And a month after the conflict started *Pravda* said:

> Peace and friendship between the U.S.S.R. and Germany are also in the interest of all nations of Europe. Conditions of anxiety, enmity and mutual distrust in Eastern Europe are advantageous only for warmongers who are used to make others pull chestnuts out of the fire for them. Such conditions were maintained in the course of many years by a policy of incitement of one country against the other.[30]

Professor Harry Elmer Barnes in reply to the charge of bellicosity of the German people says:

> England has been way out in front in point of relative bellicosity among the nations, while Germany and the Netherlands stand at the very bottom of the list, next to Denmark.

This conclusion is forced by such findings as those in Professor Quincy Wright's *A Study of War* wherein it is shown that in the period from 1480 to 1940 there were 278 wars involving European countries, whose percentage participation was as follows:

"England, 28; France, 26; Spain, 23; Russia, 22; Austria, 19; Turkey, 15; Poland, 11; Sweden, 9; Italy, 9; Netherlands, 8; Germany [including Prussia], 8; and Denmark, 7," [Vol. I, p. 221]

Likewise Pitirim Sorokin, in Vol. III, Part II of his *Social and Cultural Dynamics*, shows that from the twelfth century to 1925 the percentage of years in which leading European powers have been at war is as follows [p. 352]:

Country	Percent of Years at War
Spain	67
Poland	58
England	56
France	50
Russia	46
Holland	44
Italy	36
Germany	28

Sorokin concludes, therefore, "that Germany has had the smallest and Spain the largest per cent of years at war." Of leading modern European states England, France, and Russia thus show nearly twice the bellicosity displayed by the "war-loving" Germans.

Prof. Barnes goes on:

> President Truman has well said that constructive public acts must be based on truth. It is too bad somebody could not have whispered a little truth into his ear before he left for Potsdam. There is little prospect that a structure erected wholly on lies in 1945 will endure any better than the one that was wholly based on lies in 1919.
>
> And the probability is that the disillusionment after Potsdam will set in much more rapidly than it did after Versailles. In the period after 1919, we had to wait some years to obtain formerly secret documents to upset the lies of the period of war and peacemaking. This time, the upsetting facts are already available and so clear that any honest and informed man can read them while running. The only thing that we have to wait for is courage enough to state what is today well known and above serious doubt—in short, to know that an honest historian will not be listed immediately as a defendant in a mass sedition trial.[31]

Incitement to war is a terrible thing. Oliver Lyttleton, British Minister of Production, told the Chamber of Commerce of America in London, June 20, 1944, as reported by the United Press:

> Japan was provoked into attacking the United States at Pearl Harbor. It is a travesty on history ever to say that America was forced into the war.[32]

It is now established that to avoid war with the United States, Germany ordered its submarines not to retaliate in any way when attacked by U.S. forces under orders from Washington. In clear violation of international law our vessels in the Atlantic were ordered two months before Pearl Harbor to shell all Axis craft encountered. At the time, Admiral Stark had sent a message to Admiral Kimmel that "we are at war" in the Atlantic.

Two months after Pearl Harbor, Prime Minister Churchill told the House of Commons:

> When I survey and compute the powers of the United States and its vast resources and feel that they are now in it with us, with British Commonwealth of Nations all together, however long it lasts, till death or victory, I cannot believe that there is any other fact in the whole world which can compare with that. That is what I had dreamed of, aimed at, and worked for, and now it has come to pass.[33]

Our lend-lease program had been squeezed through Congress by the narrowest of margins as a "peace measure." Senator Glass had given away its real purpose, however, when he said he favored loaning Great Britain all the war equipment we could spare "to wipe Germany off the face of the map.[34] He had the courage to say what was on the mind of many a figure in Washington and elswhere.

Hitler has been condemned as a violator of international pacts and agreements; yet when we sent destroyers to Britain long before Pearl Harbor and later on permitted many of our vessels to be commandeered by British officers we violated Section 3 of Article V of the Act of June 15, 1917, which provides that during a war in which the United States is a neutral nation, it shall be unlawful to send out of the jurisdiction of the United States any vessel built, armed, or equipped as a vessel of war with any intent or with reasonable cause to believe that it shall be used by any belligerent nation. We also violated the Hague Convention which forbids a neutral nation to supply any war materials whatever to any belligerent country.

There is no need to pursue the argument further. We have shown that good grounds exist for doubting in some degree, at least, the charge that the German people, because of their perverse natures, and their will and lust for war, were the sole culprits in the late conflict. There is equal room, therefore, for doubting the Justice of the Potsdam program to cripple Germany and condemn its people to perpetual poverty, and equally sound moral grounds for the repudiation of that program.

On "Collective Guilt" and Propaganda

The victors in every war think they are right and the defeated wrong. The late war has offered no exception. By continuing to condemn the defeated in this war as a race of criminals and punishing them accordingly, as we at first set out to do, we would be setting a most dangerous precedent, one which our children might have good reason to regret. For if we should ever lose a war we could only expect similar treatment.

It is manifestly unjust to blame and punish the people of any country for the acts of their leaders, especially where the people have been brought under the heel of a dictatorship which under heavy penalty compels conformity to the leaders's edicts and orders.

The truth is that the people of no nation in modern history, including ourselves, have ever enjoyed an important voice in the making of the great decisions either of going to war or of framing the peace arrangements. This is one of the greatest facts we must face. America cannot possibly add amelioration to the sordid game of power politics which has plunged the nations of the world into one terrible war after another, until the people do assert themselves and insist upon the injection of justice into the peace arrangements.

But before this can be accomplished they must break the bonds of false propaganda. This propaganda flows from two major levels, a higher and a lower. Britain's pose as upholder of righteousness while actually engaged in manipulating the balance of power system exemplifies the upper level. This type of propaganda is poignantly described by the late John Maynard Keynes in *The Economic Consequences of The Peace*:

> The politics of power are inevitable and there is nothing very new to learn about this war or the end it was fought for; England had destroyed, as in each preceding century, a trade rival; a mighty

chapter had been closed in the secular struggle between the glories of Germany and of France. Prudence required some measure of lip service to the "ideals" of foolish Americans and hypocritical Englishmen, but it would be stupid to believe that there is much room in the world, as it really is, for such affairs as the League of Nations or any sense in the principle of self-determination, except as an ingenious formula for rearranging the balance of power in one's own interests.

This was written about World War I, but it applies as well to the second. Another Englishman, the great Disraeli, said:

> All great events have been distorted, most of the important causes concealed, some of the principal characters never appear, and all who figure are so misunderstood and misrepresented that the result is a complete mystification. If the history of England is ever written by one who has the knowledge and the courage, the world would be astonished.[35]

British Foreign Minister Ernest Bevin told the truth about the propaganda of the lower level when he said at the London Conference of Foreign Ministers, February 10, 1946:

> A newspaper has three things to do. One is to amuse, another is to entertain, and the rest is to mislead.[36]

That such propaganda has played an enormous part in fomenting most wars cannot be doubted. It deceives and bewilders the public, inflaming it and strengthening its innate prejudices which civilizing processes ordinarily hold to tolerable proportions. People can accurately judge only those things which come within the purview of their direct experience or which they are allowed to view from all angles by education processes. When the mediums upon which the people rely to bring them their foreign news, color and emasculate the facts, or even manufacture them out of whole cloth, as they sometimes do, there is no possiblity for the public to get the truth. Its collective judgment, the accuracy of which is the base upon which democratic processes rest, cannot, in consequence, be reliable; on the contrary, if its judgment is misled and its passions inflamed properly for the purpose, it will inevitably support mad adventures, unjust interventions, and other tragic missteps in international affairs.

Thus, Prime Minister Neville Chamberlain, a month before war broke out, sadly observed:

> Unhappily, bad feeling between nations is fomented daily by poisonous propaganda in the press and by other means. I cannot help feeling that if only we halt this war of words and some action is taken which would tend to restore confidence of the people in the peaceful intentions of all the statesmen of Europe—if only that could be done, then I still feel that I know of no question that could not and should not be solved by peaceful discussions. The gain would be enormous. On the other hand, if war should come, whichever side may claim ultimate victory, nothing is more certain that victor and vanquished alike would glean a gruesome harvest of human misery and suffering.[37]

Americans, as well as the British, were flooded with misleading, inflamatory propaganda on the eve of the war. Only a few calm, informed observers were able, apparently, to see through it. In a letter to Hugh W. Long & Co., an executive of Roosevelt & Son of Pine Street, wrote, six months before we were plunged into war:

> I cannot refrain from expressing my contempt for those who are politically toying with the fear motif at this time and painting a picture of the United States overrun by Adolf Hitler. There never was a country so strongly situated strategically for defense as this one, and when, in addition, that country has more oil than any other country in the world and more practical inventive achievements to its credit (including the original invention of and most of the significant improvements upon the airplane), and has an established and recognized aptitude for mass production, it is clear to me that it has a special genius for mechanized warfare and that all talk about what Adolf Hitler's armed forces may to do us is just bunk.
>
> No, if totalitarianism is coming to the United States it will come because the American people can be charmed by insincere, superficial, adroit politicians and fail to demand the leadership of men of character, of courage, of honesty.[38]

Perhaps the most poisonous of all the propaganda themes circulated in this country in full page newspaper ads and elsewhere was the purported statement of Adolf Hitler that he was going to come over here some day and finish off "decadent Yankeedom." The passage was dressed up to look like a direct quotation and was placed over the name of Adolf Hitler. Every effort was made to give the impression that it came from *Mein Kampf*; whereas, it was something Hermann Rauschning had said Hitler had said—the unsupported testimony of one man, a refugee.

Such a proposition is quite at variance with what Hitler actually wrote in *Mein Kampf* where he decries Germany's vulnerability on account of her exposed borders and the small extent of her national territory and extolls the United States on account of "its vast space, which is equivalent to the size of a Continent" and its "incomparable inner strength." The gigantic North American State," he says, "with the enormous resources of its soil, is much more invulnerable that the encircled German Reich." Again he says:

> Military decisions are more quickly, more easily, more completely and more effectively gained against States which have extensive territories. Moreover, the magnitude of a national territory is of itself a certain assurance that an outside power will not hastily risk the adventure of an invasion; for in that case the struggle for power would have to be long and exhausting before victory could be hoped for. The risk being so great, there would have to be extraordinary reasons for such an aggressive adventure. Hence it is that the territorial magnitude of a State furnishes a basis whereon national liberty and independence can be maintained with relative ease . . .[39]

Yet, how firmly propaganda had fixed the public impression that *Mein Kampf* offered a program for world conquest is brought out in the following excerpt taken from the transcript of the question period following an address given by Ambassador John Cudahy before the Chicago Council of Foreign Relations a month and a half before Pearl Harbor.

> Chairman Bentley: I have a question here in writing: "How do you reconcile Hitler's announced plan of world conquest with his statements made to you?"
>
> Mr. Cudahy: I know of no plan of world conquest. (Cries of "How about *Mein Kampf*?" from audience).
>
> I read *Mein Kampf* very thoroughly and I cannot find any plan of world conquest. (Cries of Oh-h-h-h from audience). It used to put me to sleep; but after I had been in Germany I read the thing very thoroughly. Hitler has made a number of statements that would indicate that he has dreamed of world empire, but I guess Hitler can be guilty of a bit of campaign oratory.
>
> . . . . I know that this war was caused by the last war.

There never was any actual evidence that world conquest was contemplated. General Marshall, Army Chief of Staff, in his biennial report released in October, 1945, stated that valuation by the War Department General Staff of interrogations of ranking members of the Germany high command had "failed to disclose any over-all German strategic plan to conquer the world.[40]

Conclusion

The Allied program to reeducate the Germans is a case of one deluded group trying to disillusion another. Our conviction that the Germans have been filled with poisonous propaganda is quite correct and our impulse to extirpate the effects of that propaganda is a good one. However, we cannot accomplish our purpose when so many of our own ideas are false, and especially when the Germans know from direct experience that they are false. To be successful a teacher must enjoy the respect of those he attempts to teach. He must win that respect through the demonstrated superiority of his knowledge and understanding. Part of what we are trying to teach the Germans is true and could have a most salutary effect on the German outlook, if only we could get the Germans to listen with respect and sympathy. But too much of what we try to make them believe the Germans know to be untrue, and this knowledge on their part causes them to lose their respect for us and to turn a deaf ear to everything we say.

Our reeducation program should begin at home. If we could only overcome the effects of our own illusions born of propaganda and ignorance arising from lack of intimate knowledge of European affairs, if we could only possess ourselves of the facts and then face them courageously, we not only could reeducate the Germans but could eliminate many erroneous and tragically dangerous features of our German program. Unless we do revise our own ideas and the program to which those ideas have given birth, we are in danger of losing Germany, Europe, and everything for which we fought this costly war. It is hoped that this book will help point the way to truth and therefore to our future success.

Our experience in Europe has already taught us some bitter lessons and has forced us to ameliorate in some degree the harsh and brutal program which we set about to force upon our defeated enemy. But we have much more to learn and must make many more changes in our policy before we can hope for the success of our German adventure. With these facts in mind we offer the following suggestions.

A Brief Plan for Germany

Rush emergency food supplies to Germany. Raise the base diet to 2,200 calories per person per day immediately, and to 2,500 calories during the winter. Permit the Central Red Cross to function. Remove all limitations to private relief. Organize great drives under the sponsorship of Government, if possible, to provide clothing, fuel, medicines, and other necessities now lacking.

Free all German war prisoners, return them to Germany, and provide them with the tools needed so they can work in Germany to feed and otherwise provide for the German people, and thereby remove a heavy burden from our shoulders. Give all prisoners full union wages for work extracted from them since V-E Day, to enable them to reestablish themselves and provide for their surviving dependents.

Return all German lands and restore the Reich's 1937 borders. Hold plebiscites in all other territories heavily populated by Germans in 1937, Danzig and Austria included, to determine, in harmony with the Atlantic Charter, under what flag these peoples wish to live.

To relieve the present unbearable population pressure, encourage all countries with low population densities, such as the United States, Canada, Latin America, Australia, and Africa to lower the bars and permit the excess German population to emigrate.

Extend all possible aid to rebuild German cities, restore essential public services, and create decent housing facilities.

Remove all limitations to industrial production and encourage highest possible output (except munitions), in harmony with the thesis that "prosperity, like peace, is indivisible."

Encourage German foreign trade in order to enable the Germans to maintain themselves as soon as possible. Place a value on the mark in terms of other currencies to make private German foreign trade possible. Permit production and operation of commercial ariships and ocean-going vessels.

Rehabilitate national finances and forestall inflation by stabilizing the currency. Contract existing currency by calling in outstanding marks and exchanging them for new marks on some such basis as five old for one new, and make all debts and contracts payable in the new marks at the same ratio in place of the old. Let experts decide the exact ration needed for this operation which will aim to bring the price level down to that of 1937. Thereafter changes in the total supply of means of payment should be made to correspond to changes in national capacity to produce.

Lower taxes to revive incentives and the profit motive.

Remove all limitations on scientific research and invention, with prohibitions continued only in the fields of atomic fission, poison gas, and weapons of war.

Allow the Germans to set up a unified, central government of their own choosing, in harmony with the Atlantic Charter, with only such external controls as those mentioned below. Encourage the Germans to frame a Constitution for themselves, with all parties advocating dictatorship or revolution barred from the Constitutional Convention.

Thereupon, withdraw all occupation troops, remove the military governments, and abolish all zones. Continue disarmament permanently, however and prohibit production of munitions and all weapons of war. To enforce United Nations controls install a system of observation and surprise inspection by roving patrols, permitted to inspect any and all records and activities, and backed by the military might of the United States and other United Nations. Violators to be tried before German courts by Allied prosecutors, with verdicts subject to appeal and retrial, if necessary, before Allied tribunals.

Insist on abolition of all discrimination in favor of displaced persons and others, and make all persons in Germany equal before the law.

Withdraw the reeducation program as gracefully and soon as possible. Replace the general anti-Nazi decrees with specific laws forbidding propagation and advocacy of certain clearly defined and specified ideas or activities, making these prohibitions apply to all alike, including Communists, so that if a certain principle previously advocated by the Nazis and outlawed as socially dangerous, happens also to be advocated by the Communists, the suppression will apply to Communists and all others alike, and not just to former Nazis as at present. Abolish all other edicts establishing political discrimination and give former Nazis a chance to reestablish themselves as productive, respectable, law abiding citizens with full rights. Abolish all censorship and facilitate intercourse between the Germans and the outside world. Permit Germans to travel freely to other countries and citizens of other countries to visit Germany as they wish.

Only by such an example of wisdom and humanity, can we teach the Germans effectively the advantages of our ways of life. By advancing such a program and pressing for its acceptance by our allies, we could instantly win the support and sympathy of virtually all Germans. Russia's designs on Germany would be frustrated, war between East and West would be unnecessary, the world would be spared another tragic holocaust.

Reference Notes

Chapter One

1. Associated Press, New York, June 3, 1945.
2. J. Kingsbury Smith, Paris, Feb. 24, 1945, [INS].
3. Cf. address by Donald M. Nelson, Chr. U.S. Production Board, Toronto, Canada. July 8, 1943; James D. White, *Chicago Daily News* [AP], May 7, 1945; and *Chicago Sunday Tribune*, Sept. 22, 1946, reporting statement by Troyer S. Anderson, War Dept. Historian.
4. Henry T. Gorrell [UP], *Chicago Daily News*, Nov. 17, 1944.
5. Associated Press, London, June 11, 1945.
6. Eddie Gilmore [AP], Berlin, June 9, 1945.
7. United Press, London, Feb. 14, 1945 and Associated Press, London, March 5, 1945.
8. Associated Press, London, March 24, 1945.
9. Jack Bell, *Chicago Daily News* Foreign Service, Kassel, Germany, May 15, 1946.

Chapter Two

1. Karl Brandt, "The Rehabilitation of Germany," address Oct. 11, 1944, Chicago Council of Foreign Relations.
2. Brought out by U.S. Secretary of State Byrnes in speech at Stuttgart, Germany, Sept. 6, 1946.
3. Hal Foust, Berlin, July 14, 1946, *Chicago Tribune* Press Service.
4. August 16, 1945, as reported by E.R. Noderer, *Chicago Tribune* Press Service.
5. Quoted by Sen. Homer Capehart in speech before U.S. Senate, Feb. 5, 1946.
6. Same source as No. 5.
7. Statement to press conference August 22, 1946, in Washington, D.C., as reported by John Fisher, *Chicago Tribune* Press Service.
8. *Chicago Tribune* Press Service, Stockholm, Sweden, Dec. 13, 1945.
9. Henry Wales, Berlin, Nov. 18, 1945, *Chicago Tribune* Press Service.
10. *Congressional Record*, Dec. 4, 1945, p. 11554, and *New York Daily News*, October 8, 1945.
11. *Chicago Herald American*, April 1, 1945, p. 16.
12. *Chicago Daily Tribune*, March 14, 1946.

Chapter Three

1. Associated Press, Moscow, March 31, 1945.
2. Quoted in *Congressional Record,* March 29, 1946, p. 2864.
3. Cf. David Dallin, *The Real Soviet Russia* (Yale University Press, 1944), Chapter XI, "Forced Labor."
4. Hal Foust, Berlin, Sept. 17, 1946, *Chicago Tribune* Press Service.
5. Hal Foust, Berlin, Aug. 11, 1946, *Chicago Tribune* Press Service.
6. Hal Foust, Berlin, Aug. 19, 1946, *Chicago Tribune* Press Service.
7. Hal Foust, Berlin, June 5, 1946, *Chicago Tribune* Press Service.
8. Associated Press, Stockholm, Nov. 30, 1945.
9. *Chicago Tribune* Press Service, Geneva, Switzerland, Sept. 15, 1946.
10. John Thompson, Geneva, Switzerland, Aug. 24, 1946, *Chicago Tribune* Press Service.
11. *The Progressive,* Jan. 14, 1946, p. 4.
12. Louis Clair, *The Progressive,* Jan. 14, 1946.
13. *Congressional Record,* Dec. 11, 1945, p. A-5816.
14. Henry Wales, Paris, March 12, 1946, *Chicago Tribune* Press Service.
15. *Chicago Tribune* Press Servie, Lille, France, July 6, 1946.
16. John Thompson, Geneva, Aug. 18, 1946, *Chicago Tribune* Press Service.
17. John Thompson, Geneva, Aug. 24, 1946, *Chicago Tribune* Press Service.
18. Arthur Veysey, London, May 28, 1946, *Chicago Tribune* Press Service.
19. Arthur Veysey, London, May 8, 1946, *Chicago Tribune* Press Service.
20. Same as No. 19.
21. Same as No. 18.
22. Ward Walker, London, March 7, 1946, *Chicago Tribune* Press Service.
23. *Chicago Tribune* Press Service, London, May 19, 1946.
24. *Chicago Tribune* Press Service, London, Aug. 27, 1946, and*The Chicago Sun* , Aug. 27, 1946 (London AP dispatch).
25. John Wilhelm, London, Sept. 12, 1946,*The Chicago Sun* London Bureau.
26. Same as No. 10.
27. Same as No. 10.
28. *Chicago Tribune* Press Service, Geneva, Switzerland, May 30, 1946.
29. Same as No. 18.
30. Henry Wales, Geneva, Switzerland, April 13, 1946,*Chicago Tribune* Press Service.
31. Same as No. 30.
32. *Chicago Daily Tribune* , March 14, 1946.
33. Cf.*The Progressive* , Feb. 4, 1945, p. 1.
34. *Vital Speeches* , May 15, 1946. p. 480.
35. *National Legionaire* , Feb. 1945.
36. James M. Haswell, Washington, Aug. 27, 1946, *Chicago Daily News* , Washington Bureau.

34. United Press, Washington, Jan. 3, 1941.
35. *Congressional Record,* Dec. 11, 1945, p. A-5815.
36. Associated Press, London, Feb. 10, 1946.
37. David Darrah, London, July 31, 1939, *Chicago Tribune* Press Service.
38. Roosevelt and Son, 30 Pine St., N.Y., to Hugh W. Long and Co., 155 Exchange Place, Jersey City, N.J., May 8, 1941.
39. *Mein Kampf* (London: Hurst and Blackett, Ltd., 1939), p. 125. Cf. also pp. 127, 463, and 520.
40. Walter Trohan, Washington, Oct. 9, 1945, Chicago Tribune Press Service.